American diaspora : poetry of displaceme

American Diaspora

American

POETRY OF DISPLACEMENT

Diaspora

Edited by **VIRGIL SUÁREZ & RYAN G. VAN CLEAVE**

UNIVERSITY OF IOWA PRESS **ψ** *Iowa City*

University of Iowa Press, Iowa City 52242
Printed in the United States of America
http://www.uiowa.edu/~uipress

The publication of this book was generously supported by the
University of Iowa Foundation.

Printed on acid-free paper

Library of Congress Cataloging-in-Publication Data
American diaspora: poetry of displacement / edited by Virgil
Suárez and Ryan G. Van Cleave.
    p.   cm.
    Includes index.
ISBN 0-87745-746-8 (cloth), ISBN 0-87745-747-6 (pbk.)
    1. American poetry.   2. Emigration and immigration—
Poetry.   3. Migration, Internal—Poetry.   4. Moving,
Household—Poetry.   5. Loss (Psychology)—Poetry.
6. Immigrants—Poetry.   7. Refugees—Poetry.   I. Suárez,
Virgil, 1962–.   II. Van Cleave, Ryan G., 1972–.
PS595.E54 A45   2001
811.009'353—dc21

                        00-053641

01 02 03 04 05 C 5 4 3 2 1
01 02 03 04 05 P 5 4 3 2 1

Contents

III. INVOCATIONS

Editors' Note

From the inception of our idea for *American Diaspora: Poetry of Displacement*, we wanted to delve deeply into the most personal of topics: home. The United States is mobile. We have commuter flights. We have fleets of taxi cabs. We have fast food. We have drive-through wedding chapels. In a culture so dominated by speed and movement, it's no wonder that when we finally stop and take stock of our lives we are distanced, fragmented, uprooted, lost.

To fully explore the concept of diaspora, we broadened the scope of our definition to include not only the physical act of moving and immigration — on which America is founded — but also the spiritual and emotional components, which can still occur — if we look to Emily Dickinson and other poets — in a life spent entirely in one location. As the poems in this anthology indicate, the United States is a nation in self-exile, its people carried on waves of anonymity and yearning. Diaspora, for us, constitutes a powerful definition for the modern condition of contemporary Americans, particularly for poets, who speak for the psyche of America.

We fell in love with both the word and the idea of diaspora because it has a raspiness to it. Over the years, we heard poets talking at conferences, over telephone lines, and via their extended family and friends — talking, tirelessly, of places they've left behind, places they inhabit now, places they yearn to be. Recently at a reading in Tallahassee, novelist Robert Olen Butler spoke of characters' "yearning" in successful stories, those stories with feeling and emotion — stories that work because they bring us closer to understanding the human condition. This same "yearning" fuels the poetry in this anthology.

Surroundings are sacred. They keep us grounded, safe, alive. Stability is found in our environment and the idea of home. For those of us who've moved often, we find solace in those connections we make to both people and places, to ways of life. We find ourselves reconnecting to our own idea of home through memory, recollection, photographs, family stories, and the archives of imagination. This has become a productive cycle for many poets. Through their work, this process of active remembering, they allow us to venture into places long forgotten, long lost.

In conversations with fellow poets and writers, we find that next to the idea of "hitting the road," there's always also the excitement of arriving at a new place, of creating a home. This is the kind of excitement immigrants who come to America share. Most of us know that it will be unknown territory, but most of us hope for a new beginning. In the fear of the unknown about a new place, there's also the hope of the future, of reinventing ourselves, of starting once again from scratch. We find it interesting that in reading and rereading F. Scott Fitzgerald's *The Great Gatsby* — a book we've both taught again recently — that this is precisely the allure of Jay Gatsby, and by extension, of Nick Carraway. Those green lights in the distance on somebody else's docks are also beckoning to us. All of us.

Much in this collection seems to have been written out of emotional necessity. These poems expose secrets, moments of exquisite power and raw beauty. These poems also expose truths, fears, dreams. Many of the poems are ambivalent, conflicted. Many are sensuous acts of remembrance and celebration. Many stem from a fundamental need to make peace with a difficult past. Still, there is the need here for approval. There is the need to understand. There is the need to reconnect and merge, to absorb, to embrace and rediscover the umbilical cord that has been severed.

Some of the poets gathered here answered invitations from us to tackle these issues of home and diaspora directly. Some we found over the years as we pored through magazines, journals, and poetry collections. It slowly came together. This book is structured in the way we thought would showcase these poems best — three simple parts called "Dislocations," "American Journeys," and "Invocations."

Some poems spoke to Virgil's own experiences with immigration, such as Gustavo Pérez Firmat's "What Hurts," Luis Rodriguez's "Running to America," G. S. Sharat Chandra's "Still Kicking in America," and Maria Mazziotti Gillan's "Arturo." Other poems dealt with Ryan's concerns over the nature of home and familial belonging, such as Stephen Corey's "Exile," Mark Jarman's "Dialect," Patty Seyburn's "Diasporadic," and Eric Pankey's "Homecoming." Still other poems surprised us, and wonderfully so, by ranging far and wide to uncover more of the emotional and spiritual ground that diaspora covers.

Poets like R. T. Smith, Toi Derricotte, Ray Gonzalez, C. Dale Young, Christopher Davis, Timothy Liu, Vivian Shipley, Sherod Santos, Heather Sellers, and many others teach us new ways of thinking about exile. Their work is exalting and becomes a poignant testimony to what it means to be an American. Kim Addonizio, Patricia Goedicke, Reginald Gibbons, Albert Goldbarth, Wendy Bishop, and Ed Ochester dazzle us not only with language but with powerful visions of ourselves in the great divide of our lives. Most of these poets will make you come back time and again, as we find ourselves doing, because their work offers up what all good poetry does: truth.

The endeavor of an anthology is, at best, a compromise. It seeks to harvest a generation of poetry centered around a crucial theme or ideological concern, and though this book is by no means exhaustive on the subject of diaspora and, more specifically, exile, we are pleased by the dialogue we've begun, the way one poem leaves off where another begins, how each poet adds to the community of language and camaraderie that starts the process of healing, redemption, salvation, understanding. This is precisely the reason why we want to encourage the use of this book in the classroom, as a tool to teach not only young poets but also students in general about what it means to be an American, what it means to live in a state of entropy.

This gathering of voices rises above the bluffs and dunes of our chaotic lives, the accumulation of harsh urgency that has become our existence. This book is an artifact of hope. Poets seek the way home; we urge you to listen, to follow them as they search. *Bienvenidos a casa.* Welcome home.

Virgil Suárez and Ryan G. Van Cleave
Tallahassee, Florida

Acknowledgments

We would like to thank our families for providing much-needed support during the years we spent compiling and editing this book. Our sincere thanks and heartfelt gratitude goes to Holly Carver, our wonderful editor at the University of Iowa Press, for believing that this project was as important as we knew it was. Also, and mostly, a giant thank you to all the wonderful poets who were generous not only in sharing with us their great work but also for helping us contact and solicit poetry from kindred souls in exile. Finally, we would like to thank the owners and staffs of Samrat's and Gordo's, where we spent the better part of two years with our laptops, devouring Cuban sandwiches, curry chicken, and cup-upon-cup of high-octane coffee and *cafecitos*.

During the preparation of this manuscript and for the endless daily errands, both Ryan and I would like to thank Vorgo, our tireless assistant. To this day he still won't divulge his last name. When we ask, he simply replies: "You know, there's Madonna, Gucci, Jewel . . . I'm just Vorgo." Okay, kid. We love you anyway. Thanks for all the permission calls, photocopying, filing, and computer troubleshooting.

This book is dedicated to all those who are here, there, or somewhere in between.

1. Dislocations

Dialect

MARK JARMAN

I can't remember the air, the light, the voices
Of what I used to think of as my home.
I truly can't recall how people sounded.
So now, when I hear someone on the news,
That guileless Western accent tinged with Spanish
Or vice versa, musical and flat,
Makes me ask, "What is that?" Then, I know.
And natives here will ask me when I speak,
"Where you from?" I tell them Greater Los Angeles.
A seedy, little beachtown, I say proudly,
That now, I add, has been yuppified.
I say it was a middle class, working class town
Of Anglos, Mexicans, Asians, a Black family,
Draftsmen and riveters for McDonnell-Douglas,
Hughes Aircraft, Northrop, Garrett Air Research.
Sea fog watered the morning rush hour traffic.
Kids snorkled after school and drowned at parties.
A Nike missile base protected us.
Their finned white noses sniffed the onshore breeze
And one day they were trucked off into nowhere.
From their abandoned hill we could look deep
Into the graft on graft of inland cities
And watch the riot smoke, when it erupted,
Blend with the stinging gauze of urban haze.
My parents bought their house for 20 grand.
Today, somebody else's house, it's worth
Half a million dollars – a yellow stucco
Among blue, pink, and white ones, just like it.
The colors made the sameness all seem better.
And just to cut the idyll short, the boys
Of different colors I played football with

Could turn from running plays to drawing knives
And smash each other's windshields and exchange
Curses in each other's mother tongues.
The late-night surf-crash made us all sleep soundly.
I couldn't wait to leave. But thought I'd be back.
Today rain followed snow and hammered nail holes
In the breadlike whiteness covering the heart
Of the continent's heart. All the gutters are singing.
I can't remember the air, the light, the voices.
But that's a lie. I can. Together they
Answer the reporter's questions like experts,
Surveying burning blocks by helicopter.

China Camp, California

KIM ADDONIZIO

Here's the long trough, covered by a screen,
where they cleaned shrimp.
Easier to imagine their catch
than to glimpse the ghosts of the fishermen
who lived here in these few wood buildings,
some now in need of repair, tin-roofed,
boarded windows whose gaps we peer through
to see shadowed dirt, a rusted wheelbarrow.
Of their boats, only a lone hull remains,
hauled to the sand and half-sunk there,
surrounded by chain link.
Yet everything is the same: the bay,
tamed by the curve of land that makes the cove,
still curls in
easily as hands turning over
to close, and close again, a book whose pages
ceaselessly open. Shards of their dishes
and rice bowls wash back
with the frail skeletons of crabs, glass
dulled and polished, indecipherable bits
of broken shells, jade-green kelp.
It's said they were driven out by hatred,
or concern that they'd leave nothing
for the next boats, but no one recorded
where they went. This was the home they made,
miles from China: brief shore,
a sky brushed with clouds,
gulls following them in each sunset,
the women stirring soup
with buried spoons, lost silk

of their sashes, black hair unpinned
and carried out with the tide,
tangling in the empty nets and sinking
to the coldest dark water.

Passports

PATRICIA GOEDICKE

"Naah," she says, voice too low for a wheedle
                                                too high for a sneer
            "Geez, what do we have to learn grammar for?"
                        In the 6th grade, in New Hampshire
                    end of her first year in America
            this is what it has come to:
                                        quick as a chipmunk, leggy
                    in her long American jeans
            her Maw and Paw may weep
                        over her Chinese food, out of their Chinese eyes
                        but not her, never

then what is it
        when she plays the piano
                            what is that rustle of silk
                                        I keep chasing after, bamboo groves
                            under the black fence of her hair
            the beautiful birthmark on her temple
                        like a brown rose

"Geez," she says, "Sure I'll give you music lessons,"
                        she makes me sit on the grass
                                    learn every note by sight, precise
                        patient as an ant
        after Juilliard she takes up geology
                                then microbiology
                        sterilizes chicken eggs
                            in a laboratory

earlier, reading Shaw together
                    then Mozart, then Freud,
     Shakespeare, Hemingway, Whitehead
                    while the rest of the team raced
   at field hockey we chose to be fullbacks, lounging
                    in deep grass near the goal

of course I was making it up
                    where she was going
   was no more mournfully romantic
               than it was tragic
   riding our bikes to Girl Scouts
                    in her light voice, frisky

"Heck, yes," she'd say
                  "I want to be an American"
   I would have followed her anywhere
               but there.

It was the China Sea I was after
                and music, and literature, and Art
   not Occam Pond, her father teaching religion
             to the Dartmouth Indians
               but greater waters, enormous
   smoky in her eyes

I knew she wanted to be a cheerleader
                like everyone else and couldn't
   any more than I could, with my thick glasses, my fat,
            then what was it
              the two of us aliens together
   back there when minorities
                 were still suspect

I thought what we were interested in was the mind
                              in Mexico when we traveled
                    she was more beautiful than ever
          La China Poblana
                    the Chinese citizen, they called her

but she made me take off my Girl Scout uniform for the men
                    right down to my green soul
          scared at first, then growing
                    with so many warm beds in the world
               brown muscles, yellow
eventually even white

                              what I found was my dumb Irish
                    contented self

what sort of passport
                    did she find
          when she finally went back to China was she too late
                    or too smart
                              now she throws pots
                    in Berkeley
          with two daughters and a mathematician
               for a husband

this is what it has come to
                    after twenty years in Mexico
          now I write poetry
               in Montana
          often her gold face
               weaves quizzically across mine
                              in Glacier Lake
          the Irishman I married
                    is half handsome Chinese
               half Russian Jew

Generations

KIM ADDONIZIO

Somewhere a shop of hanging meats,
shop of stink and blood, block and cleaver;

somewhere an immigrant, grandfather, stranger
with my last name. That man

untying his apron in 1910, scrubbing off
the pale fat, going home past brownstones

and churches, past vendors, streetcars, arias,
past the clatter of supper dishes, going home

to his new son, my father—
What is he to me, butcher with sausage fingers,

old Italian leaning over a child somewhere
in New York City, somewhere alive, what is he

that I go back to look for him, years after his death
and my father's death, knowing only

a name, a few scraps my father fed me?
My father who shortened that name, who hacked off

three lovely syllables, who raised American children.
What is the past to me

that I have to go back, pronouncing that word
in the silence of a cemetery, what is this stone

coming apart in my hands like bread, name
I eat and expel? Somewhere the smell of figs

and brine, strung garlic, rosemary and olives;
somewhere that place. Somewhere a boat

rocking, crossing over, entering the harbor. I wait
on the dock, one face in a crowd of faces. Souls

disembark and stream towards the city,
and though I walk among them for hours,

hungry, haunting their streets,
I can't tell which one of them is mine.

Somewhere a steak is wrapped in thick paper,
somewhere my grandmother is laid in the earth,

and my young father shines shoes on a corner,
turning his back to the old world, forgetting.

I walk the night city, looking up at lit windows,
and there is no table set for me, nowhere

I can go to be filled. This is the city
of grandparents, immigrants, arrivals,

where I've come too late with my name,
an empty plate. This is the place.

The Years

REGINALD GIBBONS

My grandmother's Russian/
English dictionary — she must
have bought it right off
the boat. I let the blue boards
fall open like lifeless wings,
the transparent book lice
scurry across
American Publishing Company
New York 1901.
                    Pulling
gently at the crumbling signatures
is like opening the door
to the attic; first,
darkness has a smell, like dust,
the summer heat leaching
wood-scent from rafters;
then, like old clothes
that were carefully folded away,
yet never meant to be worn
again after the air they were
sealed in had stopped ticking,
the angled layers of Yiddish
newspapers spill
the years into my eyes.

In the Chips

REGINALD GIBBONS

A self steps out of the self, pauses
to let his eyes adjust to the light,
reties a shoelace, and goes about
the business that you thought was yours.
You stand back and watch, you will
find something else to do.

It has happened before.
One of them did not, at the last minute,
leave home, and has worked
in a Texas bookstore all this time.
Another did not go to Spain and now
sells ointments over a counter.
A third, since the job offshore
on an oil rig, has been very ill.
A fourth, still at the Savings & Loan,
has gotten his promotion . . .
And others abound, your life continues to
branch, they have married
and bought houses, brought babies
home from hospitals, attended the funerals
of the nonexistent and the not-yet-dead.

Anyone might wonder what he
could be doing had he not
already done what he has.
Even they, with wives, when they
undress in cold rooms, in rainy winter,
and under the blankets press
their hands to breasts and their mouths
to wet night, close their eyes

on a dream of a different life —
where they see you
drum your fingertips on green felt,
feign a yawn, and turn up
a queen next to the ace, rake in
an armful of white red & blue.

Gallery

ALBERT GOLDBARTH

When my grandfather stepped from the boat
they gave him a choice of paintings to enter. "This one,"
he said by a nod of his head. Why not? — for weeks
in the bodystink quarters of steerage,
the lice had run as freely as milk through his crevices,
and the only food was saltbread softened in engine water,
but here, in *The Boating Party* by Renoir, it's spring,
the light is floral, even cloth and skin
are really petals in this light, the glass
the wine is in is alive in this light, the men are easy
in speaking with women (he noticed, oh especially,
the women), their mutual fascination is another flower
filling the air, and the clusters of fruits
looked as shining to him as an orchestra's brass section
— when he peeked around the corner of the painting, in fact,
he saw a grouse was simmering in peppered cream
and that settled it, he sat down at a nearby table,
listening to the bright and empty talk, his shy eyes
staring at his waiting plate. A server appeared
and left. On my grandfather's plate was a boiled potato,
only that. But he was starving, so he ate it. He ate it
indelicately, with an almost sexual fervor, and then
looked up to see the family around him,
with their corded hands, with their faces like worn-out shoes,
were eating theirs, just that, with a root tea. He
was in Van Gogh's *The Potato Eaters*. The room
was as dark as the tea. Outside, the wind was a punishing switch.
The talk was hushed and raw and familiar,
he was at home here, he was at home in the broken
light of the hanging oil lamp. When the meal was done,
he stepped out into the lane, he breathed the country dark in

hungrily, then walked. He needed a wife.
He needed a future. What did he see ahead,
when he squinted? He would barely understand
that man in Edward Hopper's *Nighthawks*,
on a distant corner, some depleted 3 A.M.,
was his son — who slides the dime for his java
over the counter, slants his hat, then heads out into streetlight
from the diner's unrelenting angles and planes.
He's lonely. It's 1942. He'd love to meet my mother,
someone humming a hot little tune
and pretty as a picture.

The Letter

KASEY JUEDS

He didn't want to remember Ireland,
my mother says: her grandfather

in the South Dakota mines, writing home,
happy to have so much work. She smooths his letter

so I can see. Paper thumbed to almost-transparent;
cursive careful as a child's. And nothing

about Ireland. He didn't want to remember
the country I know only from postcards —

fishing villages, ponies in fields, any stranger's
easy images. What forges sadness so insistent

he needed all those miles to keep it at bay?
My mother folds the letter, slips it away,

back into the drawer where it's lived
for years, back into the dark:

paper meager as his lamp
in the pit's extravagant black—

and just as fragile, as needed.

Exile

SANDRA CASTILLO

And you wonder how you could have decided
what to take with you for the rest of your life,
what to leave behind
— Dionisio Martinez

i.

We are gitanas,
con barajas y collares,
thinking ourselves nomads,
Hungarians, bohemians
because, sometimes, our adventures define us
as much as our props.
or so we think, my cousin Norma and I,
as we go door to door along East 4th Avenue,
a street we are not supposed to be on,
using candy as our pretext,
our costumes as our shields,
thinking we are who we want to be,
on this my first Halloween, 1970.

ii.

Pale and thin,
he stands in the middle of that icebox,
where voices cling like dishes or silverware,
like the unintelligible sounds of English,
of my voice, our trays slamming into one another,
falling on that cold-white cafeteria floor,
the green mush of American food on my lap,
his blue V-neck sweater
because I turned to look for him,
Francisco Insignari,
the first boy I consciously liked.

iii.
It is my third year in Miami:
I am in the third grade and Mr. Powers,
my angry American teacher, is telling us about Nixon,
showing us how to influence with suggestion,
how to persuade with danger,
by asking us who should be president
and countering Gonzalo, the new boy,
who alone raises his hand for McGovern,
for a chance he never got
before speech and America
because he just doesn't know
Mr. Powers.

iv.
Our classroom is called a Pod,
and we rotate to the sound of a bell.
Mr. Shuker gives us word puzzles,
from *The Miami Herald*,
Miss Christie, bride games:
"*something borrowed, something blue,*
something old, something new,"
except on Fridays, when we are taught
to speak and listen off index cards,
and have assigned cafeteria seats:
Gerardo Legra, Michael Algair,
Danny Rodgers, Maria Murgia and I.

And we sit in silence,
our conversations in our laps,
our napkins in our mouths
and we are graded on our manners,
the silence we know how to share.

v.

The first time I hear the word,
I think of breakfast:
tortilla, Cuban-style,
with onions and French fries,
on Cuban bread from the bakery on East 10th Street.

It was what my father made for us
on those days he played weekend cook,
but there was an extra syllable
that didn't make me think of Veronica,
slow dancing with Orlando's sister
to "Me & Mrs. Jones," "*Mrs. Jones, Mrs. Jones. . . .*"
though the boys gathered around her,
taunting her with what I knew couldn't be
breakfast.

vi.

Already hip at twelve,
Claro wears otherness
like a worn leather jacket I look for
down the humid-yellow halls
of Carol City Junior High,
where we are divided into shifts:
7 A.M. to 12, 12:30 to 5:30 P.M.,
where in dark corners,
he finds *amor propio*
with my closest girlfriends,
too eager to part their lips
to his popularity and my amazement
because he knows
he is my first obsession.

Diasporadic

PATTY SEYBURN

When I saw the Jews floating, I knew
it was time to pack up, when the water
struck their oak boxes, the small stones
placed atop their graves in memory
scattering, the great slabs engraved
like charms on a bracelet swept
downstream as though rocks were
driftwood, rocks were feathers —
in our game, paper bested rocks
which crippled scissors, anyway —
and I put on my tall rubber boots,
zipped my duffle that could be lifted
high as a child overhead and made
my way toward the flume — now dry,
water rising on both sides, resembling
the Red Sea's cinematic parting, smudged
extras trudging a swath of sand, pretending
that God split the sea for them clean
as a perfect center part in wet hair,
while De Mille's technicians shot Jell-o
at high-speed. I saw Jews' caskets freed
from cemetery Beth Yeshurun meandering
downtown, bumping into names, dates
and epitaphs, a few trees, I thought
oh, *we're wandering, again.* I suppose
there's no point in following the dead:
on present course, they'll run the bayous
with no regard for rapids and whitewater
chutes, careen into the Gulf, ocean-bound —
the Atlantic, the one they crossed long ago,
the Old Country newly inviting. I can't go

with them, though I was a fine swimmer
once, the one assigned the race's last leg,
who could make up time lost with long
strokes, cupped hands, strong kick, when I
turned my head for breaths I saw the others
fall behind. My distant family, my distant
lover, called for me to leave weeks ago — but
who knew that the heavens were so full?
that cumulonimbus could store centuries
of rain? No ark this time, no dove nor
olive branch, only the dry land we've made,
this slow sluice — do you see the floating Jews'
nomadic names and bodies propelled
by the waters — *now where are they going?*

On Forgettings

PATTY SEYBURN

I.

Consider the view from my bedroom window: a graveyard
brimming with Houston's oldest Jews to pass in this swelter.
Their land overlooks, filters into the bayou, adrift toward
the Gulf that submits to the ocean's tow, or gives itself away.
I took to them, invited them in across the sinuous road
where bikers dragged their grooves into the asphalt,
oblivious to the dead or living yearning for quiet.
What do I know of silence? The quiet in their wake
is worse — the harbinger of noise, and waiting is an ache
not local but broad, a hapless messenger who takes his share
of heat — we say *the wait is worse* but I say *it prepares us.*
I say *we fall in love with it and blame it for leaving.*

II.

Down West Dallas Ave. lies a freedmens' graveyard,
notched in the city street's dubious progress, stones
hardly visible, weed-doused, cloaked in a raucous tangle,
fist-sized insects and snakes driven from the Ireland
of cultivated parks. And though I wonder why no one
cleans these slate faces, why wildflowers scrawl their lines
over epitaphs, I know my indignation exists to stave off
the scarcity that I will become, the sum of name and date.
Perhaps weeds shade the sheer stones from harsh light,
save the denizens from scrutiny, vines connecting gravesites
as though beneath, the deads' hands touch: death no divorce
from yearning. We say *the wait is worse,* as though it ends.

III.

My father's cemetery is planted squarely in Detroit
where Woodward Ave. elbows 8 Mile Road — Machpelah,
named for the cave and field where Abraham rested Sarah,

and after a hundred threescore and fifteen years, found his place.
Ten years passed, this corner still uncrowded: recent dead
lie closer to where their children dwell, in suburb and exurb,
and the migrating young will need directions to trace
their attenuated names. Here, the buried lie discrete, joined
by vowel-less Hebrew, six-pointed stars — and if their hands
touch, we have no sign of it. My father drifts further and farther
into memory, his grave becoming one in a sea of stones, engraved.
We say *the wait is worse* when we mean, the forgetting.

Flood Plain: The Right-of-Way

JIM SHUGRUE

Are we ever anywhere, can we ever feel
more about a place than the desire
to come back someday when we have the time?
Displaced persons who displace
still other persons in our search for home.
We've had the place knocked out of us —
Bialistok, Ventry, Chicago —
the names we make up and the ones
we're made up of, and everywhere
the citizens of one or two
generations longer standing look
on us as interlopers, while the few
remaining, defeated, native,
can only say, "I told you so,"
in a language even their children
no longer understand. Our grandparents
could not afford to stay put:
a new way of living intruded on them
and the ground they stood on became worth more
than they were. It's the same sad song all over.
We got to Iowa with the railroads, from where,
no one remembers, and how we got out of there
is still a mystery. I learned to walk the tracks
beside my grandmother's house where the right-of-way
cut through to town, soda fountain, movies, dime store.
And so the rails stitched us together.
My grandmother had photographs of large strong women
and wiry dark men posed against the muddy hills.
Famine Irish, who like the Finns, the Chinese and all
the others, worked till they dropped and dropped like flies.
Less of an investment than slaves. They lost the market value

of chattel, to become replaceable parts. They grew up nowhere,
not even at home in their own sweat. Insular, suspicious,
maybe they never told their lies to each other, maybe
never shared each other's songs and home-brew recipes,
only fought, only shared the blood they shed, fighting,
working, making, peasants from half the world away, calling
each other by every name in the book but brother, but friend.
We are notoriously bad at discerning our real enemies.
Laying claim to absence, I will own
no region but the evicted heart.

And Wake Up Where?

DAVID LAZAR

A generation of mothers sings "Over the Rainbow" in ruby bedroom slippers. They have been inside a terrible storm, which left in its wake a dream they couldn't leave, but had to come home from.

Thirty years of fathers ask for martinis; they are shaken, but not stirred. They don't want to come home to where their pajamas hang limply in the closet like Clark Kent's backup Superman suit.

★

Perhaps after the fall comes another fall, even a little darker, as though a second daylight savings had come on. Children wait for buses, still only in little light. And some are picked up, and some are picked off in that neutral moment which isn't even exactly dawn. Better to call it a gray area, a thin line. They're taken, I think, *over the rainbow, way up high, to while away the hours, conversing with the flowers.* And all day long they can see in the distance, so far away that if they cupped their hands it would make a little screen: houses rising, houses falling, women in black with brooms beneath houses, women in black with brooms screaming curses, women with wands telling little white lies. "Why didn't you tell me I could make it home myself?" "I didn't lie. You never asked me." The biggest lie of all.

The world's become a whirling dervish, pitching our rhythm from side to side. It's that old sidereal gravity, flaunting us vertically, like a face being gently slapped with a glove. Left cheek, right cheek, left, right. *My sister, my daughter, my sister, my daughter . . .*

Wake up, little girl. You're home again. The storm has passed. Hide behind our curtains; tell us again about the men in search of missing pieces, the women with their polar powers; you, a little girl who knew so little, a girl who knew so much.

My good witch, my bad witch, my good witch, my bad witch. Use the bucket and use the shoes.

What will happen when you think back, almost a lifetime after the dream, when Kansas is in color, the great big country a kind of suburban Oz? What will happen, do you think, when the voice of your mind, heavy and dry with rust and straw . . . what will happen when you tell yourself to say, *There was no place like home, there was no place . . .*

Political or Not, Here Comes That Poem

WENDY BISHOP

Number of times the phrase "happens to be black"
has appeared in the New York Times since January
1990: 17.
— Harper's Index, November 1991, p. 17

My mother, who happens to be dead,
had little or nothing to say about
her country, which happened to be
the United States. We were not political
in that living room middle-class way,
which happened to center on the new
television and phonograph console:
eight-inch screen imbedded in a cheap
hotel blond wood, tuned-in to vague
men in hats, who happened to be concerned
in world events — a cold war, a hot war,
military finance, CIA and G-men — reported
by more hat-men holding microphones
the size of scepters. My father,
who also happens to be dead, had Army
things to say about his country,
which happened to be the U.S. of A.
and jumbled memories of Army base PXes
in Germany, Japan and the Fort Lewis, WA.
His hat waves to me, a green flap of military
gabardine that fell silent like a mouth
or perched on orderly hair. His demands
were reasonable: A home darkroom, a German
Shepherd dog, daughters who tied their
hair back at dinner, which happened to take place
about six P.M., and remained hysterically bland
for two decades–canned peas and meatloaf
took us from the gravy-days of the fifties

to the sixties and my parents, who were
struggling in a peculiarly American way,
couldn't understand: The phonograph console
blew jazz before rock: The neighbors who
moved in just happened to be Cuban:
The boys daughters dated might happen to be
black. And the president was shot, was shot,
was shot; all the CIA hat-men couldn't
think of a thing to say to the shrunken
microphones of the newspaper men
who were turning even then into women.
My sisters happened to get married
and I happened to go on to school
to get certified to write poems about writing
homeless poems about writing ecology poems
about writing political poems
in a moment I'll write that poem
which just happens to be thinking a little
too much: it runs by screaming
like an assassination siren
or the serviceable plaid pattern of our lives.

Changing the Name to Ochester

ED OCHESTER

When other grandpas came to Ellis Island
the Immigration people asked "Name?"
and they said "Sergius Bronislaus Jygzywglywcz"
and the officer said "ok, from now on your name's
Sarge Jerko," and Sarge trundled off to the Lower East Side
with a lead cross and a sausage wrapped in a hair shirt
and shared a tiny ill-lit room with eight *Landleute*
and next to a pot of boiling diapers began to carve
yo-yos to peddle on the street and forty years later
was Sarge Jerko, Inc., the Yo-Yo King,
but my grandfather was born in this country
(no one living knows anything about his parents)
and was an engineer for Con Edison
when he married the immigrant girl
Katherina Humrich who everybody said
was once very pretty but when I knew her
had a tight bun, thin German lips
and a nose which came to her chin;
her major pleasures were trips to Coney Island
with friends and frightening little children
by jumping out from behind curtains, after which
she cackled hilariously. This is all I know for certain
about my grandfather: 1) his name was Olshevski,
and he changed it shortly after his marriage,
when they were living in an Irish neighborhood,
2) while working at Con Ed he bought a yacht
my grandmother said, but my mother said "Mom,
it was just a boat," 3) he left Katherina
after the fourth son was born, and she lived
in a tiny apartment on Chauncy Street
which smelled, even when I was eight,

like boiled diapers, 4) he was reported
to be handsome and have "a roving eye,"
5) my father and his brothers
all of whom are dead now
refused to go to his funeral
and never spoke of him.

This is a poem about forgiving Grandpa
for my not knowing him. And father, if you're
reading over my shoulder, I don't forget how
you had three cents spending money a week
and gave two cents to the church, or how
Uncle George, the baby who was everybody's
darling, couldn't go to college because he had
to work to support the family like everybody else
and how he became a fire chief in the City of Nueva York,
and how Uncle Will, before he died of cancer,
became an advisor to La Guardia and made a bundle
by being appointed trustee of orphans' estates,
or how Uncle Frank, driving his battery truck
once was stopped by Will and La Guardia in their big car
and they chatted, and Uncle Frank — my favorite uncle,
neither Olshevski nor Ochester — still talks
about how his partner Paddy kept saying
"Bejasus, it was the Mayor,"
or how because you had to support your brothers
you couldn't marry till 30
and were engaged for eight years to my mother
who to this day loves you because you did
what you had to do, and how you built your business
going door-to-door selling insurance on Chauncy Street
and Myrtle Avenue till late at night, arguing and collecting
quarters and dimes from people who lived in tiny apartments
smelling of boiled diapers.
Nearly twenty years since your death, father,

and long ago I've forgiven you, and I think
you did love me really, and who am I, who was born
as you said "with everything," to condemn
your bitterness toward your father who left you
as you said "with nothing"?

I don't believe in original sin.
I believe if we're strong enough and gather our powers
we could work it out: no petty human misery,
no windrows of the dead slaughtered
in suicide charges, no hearts shrunken
and blackened like meat spitted
and held too long to the fire.
But what everybody knows
is enough to make you laugh
and to break your heart.
Grandpa, forty years after your death,
by the power invested in me as the oldest
living Ochester in the direct line I hereby
forgive you. And though you died,
my mother says, penniless and alone
with no one to talk to
I hope that when you abandoned your family
you lived well. I hope you sailed your 15-foot
yacht out into Long Island Sound
with a pretty woman on board and a bottle
of plum brandy. I hope that when the huge yacht
with "Jerko II" on the stern sailed by
you looked up and said "honey,
you'll be sailing one like that some day"
and that she giggled and said "yeah,
hon, gimme a kiss" and afterwards tilted
the bottle, and that the sun was shining
on the Sound, and that you enjoyed
the bitter smell of the brine and

the brilliance of the white scud and
that when you made love that night
it was good and lasted
a long, long time.

José Canseco Breaks Our Hearts Again

GUSTAVO PÉREZ FIRMAT

Out for the season, what's new.
31 homers, best in the AL, 71 RBIs,
and a herniated disk.

David had asked me to tape the home-run derby
and now he says not to bother.
Stupid me, I worry that with Canseco

laid up, my son and I will not have something to talk about.
José has missed one-third of his career,
over 500 games, or he'd have 600 homers by now.

I think of all the sentences
David and I could have said to each other
if José's back did not keep giving out on us.

(He had to be Cuban, that impossible man-child,
delicate as an orchid beneath the rippling chest.)

I'll keep my fingers crossed for next season
when José, like a certain country I know,
will break our hearts again.

Poem for Pancho Gonzales

LEROY V. QUINTANA

This was the world of white lines, a game
unlike any other, where the object was to win,
only you used words like "Please"
if your aim ended up improperly
in the next court, "Thank you" when
the ball was returned and "Love"
after you scored first.

Yours was the name that survived
the hatred only California can inspire,
strong enough to be etched in fire
on tennis rackets redeemed
by thrifty mothers who built a life
on S&H Green Stamps a dish,
a dish, a lamp, an ashtray at a time.

Running to America

LUIS RODRIGUEZ

They are night shadows
Violating borders.
Fingers curled through chain-link fences,
Hiding from infra-red eyes,
Dodging 30-30 bullets,
They leave familiar smells,
Warmth and sounds,
As ancient as the trampled stones.

Running to America.

There is a woman in her finest
Border-crossing wear:
A purple blouse from an older sister,
A pair of worn shoes
From a church bazaar,
A tattered coat from a former lover.

There is a child dressed in black,
Fear sparkling from dark Indian eyes,
Clinging to a headless Barbie doll.

And the men, some hardened, quiet,
Others young and loud—
You see something like this in prisons.

Soon they will cross on their bellies,
Kissing black earth,
Then run to America.

City of Angels

LUIS RODRIGUEZ

Somewhere out there lies the city.
Bare breasted. Awaiting my return.
This is the city of abandoned nights,
of six-year-olds falling through rusted fire escapes,
of welfare hotels in facades of diseased stone —
the city of grit, wood, and bone. I step out of a foul-smelling Greyhound bus
into the mouth of a moistened dawn,
spraying its colors on cardboard "condos"
on the sidewalk.
Here I stroll among the walking dead,
among the criminalized and displaced —
the sun of the desert our only roof
the song of our wails,
the wails of our song,
thundering against the sides
of this city of angels
so far removed from heaven.

The Emigrant

KATHERINE SÁNCHEZ

I am the boy, stomach flat on sand.
I reach under the barbed wire fence
for homeland dirt. The soldier's boot
smooths the wrinkles on my hand like an iron.

I am the child, jumping on the new
leather sofa. I laugh at the poster
on the living room wall of the boy
touching homeland dirt.

I am the man, watching the child.
The money is gone. My teeth
burden my mouth like chiseled
gravestones. My tongue
is a dried rose. If I speak,
it will crumble.

I am the homeland.
Your family sings
in my quicksand.

Willie and the Train

CARISSA NEFF

Willie Carsten opens the bakery early
as the train rattles down the track outside.

We are watching him make pretzels and cakes,
waiting for free bread.

Willie tells my papa I'm too old to suck my thumb.
Papa says he knows, looks at Mama,
clears his throat uneasily.

We know all the Germans.
They play pinochle
and eat potato pancakes
in the basement of St. John's Lutheran church.

My papa points outside.
Says that if I don't stop sucking my thumb
the train will get it.

Whenever the night-trains pass
my bedroom window after that,
I cry out in fear, hold my hand in a fist
my thumb deep inside.

Each night Mama comforts me,
rocks me to the churn of the train.

I put my head between her breasts
suck my thumb anyway
take my chances
like immigrants did.

Distance

CAROLINA HOSPITAL

Distance has made of us all strangers.
Another cousin I've never met
phones mother again from Havana.
After a life of silence,
he is begging
to be flown out of the island
even on the wings of Icarus.
He calls mother *tia* and she
opens her heart, so carefully sealed
after 33 years of homesick nights.
A temporary visa and money in his pocket,
he wanders the streets of Quito, ridden with fear,
searching for the painful familiarity
he left behind.
In Lima, he is greeted by friends.
He is no longer alone.
We are sure he will make it,
wait his turn to reach us.
No.
Carlos has gone home,
back to Havana,
to his wife and daughter
and the habitual echoes of empty rooms.

Mi Vida: *Wings of Fright*

MARTÍN ESPADA

— *Chelsea, Massachusetts*

The refugee's run
across the desert borderlands
carved wings of fright
into his forehead,
growing more crooked
with every eviction notice
in this waterfront city of the north.

He sat in the office for the poor,
daughter burrowed asleep
on one shoulder,
and spoke to the lawyer
with a voice trained obedient
in the darkness of church confessionals
and police barracks, Guatemalan dusk.

The lawyer nodded through papers,
glancing up only when the girl awoke
to spout white vomit on the floor
and her father's shirt.
"*Mi vida:*" My life, he said,
then said again, as he bundled her
to the toilet.

This is how the lawyer,
who, like the fortune-teller,
had a bookshelf of prophecy
but a cabinet empty of cures,
found himself
kneeling on the floor
with a paper towel.

Thieves of Light

MARTÍN ESPADA
— *Chelsea, Massachusetts, 1991*

We all knew about Gus:
the locksmith, the Edison man, and me.
We heard about the welfare hotel,
where he stacked clothes
on the sidewalk for the garbage truck
if no rent was paid by Wednesday morning.
We heard about the triple deckers,
where he heaved
someone else's chair or television
from the third floor, and raged
like a drunk blaming his woman
till the pleading tenant agreed to leave.
There was word he even shot a cop
twenty years ago, but the jury
knew Gus too, studying cuticles
or the courtroom clock
as the foreman said not guilty.
The only constable in Chelsea
wore his gun in a shoulder holster,
drooped his cigarette at a dangerous angle,
yet claimed that Gus
could not be found on Broadway
to serve a summons in his hand.

This is how we knew Gus:
Luisa saw the sludge pop
from the faucet, the mice
dropping from the ceiling,
shook her head and said no rent,
still said no after his fist

buckled the bolted door.
In the basement, Gus hit switches.
The electric arteries in the walls
stopped pumping, stove cold,
heat off, light bulbs gray.
She lived three months in darkness,
the wax from her candle spreading
over the kitchen table like a calendar
of the constant night,
sleeping in her coat, a beggar
in the underworld kingdom of rodents.
When Luisa came to me, a lawyer
who knew Spanish,
she kept coughing
into her fist, apologizing
with every cough.

So three strangers
gathered in the hallway.
The locksmith
kneeled before the knob
on the basement door,
because I asked him
to be a burglar today.
The Edison man swallowed dryly,
because I asked him
to smuggle electricity today,
forget Gus's promise
of crushed fingers.
And me: the lawyer, tightly
rolling a court order in my hand
like a newspaper to swing at flies,
so far from the leatherbound books
of law school, the treatises
on the constitution
of some other country.

We worked quickly, thieves of light.
The door popped open,
as in a dream of welcome,
swaying with the locksmith's fingers.
The Edison man pressed his palms
against the fuse boxes,
and awakened the sleeping wires
in the walls. I kept watch by the door,
then crept upstairs, past Gus's office
where shadows and voices
drove the blood in my wrist
still faster. I tapped on Luisa's door.
I had to see if the light was on.

She stared at me
as if the rosary
had brought me here
with this sudden glow from the ceiling,
a stove where rice and beans
could simmer, sleep without a coat.
I know there were no angels
swimming in that dim yellow globe,
but there was a light louder than Gus,
so much light
I had to close my eyes.

Come to Find Out

JACQUELINE DEE PARKER

Might can, they say in Louisiana
when there's a distinct possibility
that performance may be achieved
or information received.
And the little engine said,
I think I might can,
I think I might can . . .
all the way to the other side of the mountain,
though there are no hills here, just wetlands
soft as a fontanel and occasional
cow patty for contour.
The doctor said,
over my big belly jelled for a sonogram,
he might could find out
the sex of my child —
Come to find out,
he was right.
Come to find out signals discovery, cognizance.
It leads the summary declarations
typically lodged in conclusions
of student composition.
Come to find out — I'd never heard it
before I lived in Louisiana.
And what about *sure don't?*
There's usually a lilting, sweet stress
on the *sure,*
a thoughtfully verbal pause
until the *don't*
falls like a nail in spongy wood.
I'm fixing to expect less when I ask questions.

This way, I might can
come to find out
more, for sure.

Poem for a Vietnamese Student

LEROY V. QUINTANA

Some words have tongues sharp as punji stakes.
They lie awake in ambush as long as necessary,
sometimes in the shadows of other words: gobbledygook.

They know the future because they have no regret
for the past. They are ill-mannered, pretend to be deaf
as clocks, in love with the sound of their names.
They lie awake in ambush as long as necessary,
sometimes in the shadow of other words: gobbledygook.

They find their way into our blood, and haunt us.
We pay with our lives all our lives.

Welcome to America. Sin loi. Get your dictionary,
go to the board, look up a new word: write down
guide words, entry word, phonetic spelling, learn
how to pronounce the word, which syllable is stressed.
Repeat after me: gobbledygook, gobbledygook, gobbledygook.

Variations for Hendrix and Vietnam

MONIFA LOVE

1
We
not White
not Yellow
corner sounds
watch death
cook a cure
we
light and high   high and light
flower blue
flower street
sip a heartful
of ocean
and spit
we
escape
longing all up in our throats
laughter
bruised laughter
all down in our bellies
We
crazy moaning lying
detonating tears   scattering petals
it smells like rain
it smells like like like
we don't know.

2
White light changes
flickers

changes at the light at H and Benning Northeast

we
watch
road weary
death cooking
we roll up
line up
shoot up
smoke
White light changes
flickers
we sit quiet with our backs
against the dark curves
of evening
nodding.

3
tears
tears
tears
for orchid brother Jamal
his road weary red lettered body
along a Pleiku hillside
his long throat
pearl belly
darkening shoulders
a circle of grey petals
at our feet

quiet.

At the Bar

RICARDO PAU-LLOSA

Germán, who swam along the coast,
Germán, who reached Guantánamo Base
over moonless surf and jagged rock,
his poems in a sealed plastic tube
strapped to his back,
Germán, who turned away
from everything Cuban
because the regime claimed it,
asks me, who sits at this bar
four times a week
to drown in the rising
smoke of awkward sacrifice,
what I get from the videos
of Cuba's golden age of music.
Before I can answer he tells me
the story of lunatics on the streets
of Guantánamo, the Cuban city north
of the Bay, where he was born.
There was a woman who lost a son
in a lightning storm and wandered
the city constantly. We called her
Juanita va a llover,
    (Juanita, it's going to rain —
    sounds like "Ahorita va a llover,"
    Soon it's going to rain,
    a refrain from a popular song).
And she would look up in terror
at any cloud, however white.
And Bemba (big lips) who could stuff
his fist in his mouth
and went from corner to corner

with a tape recorder playing
music by the Orquesta Aragón.
He would pretend to play
their dreamt instruments.
On one occasion he showed up
dressed as a samurai, complete
with kimono, cardboard sword, painted face
and Japanese sandals. Last night, I tell Germán,
a Japanese woman was singing here.
Guaguancós, no less — in Japanese, no less.
The purest of the Afro-Cuban genres,
voice and conga drums, interlaced with Basho.
It's a matter between islands, I think.
We who were born in them know intimately
the accusatory foreignness of horizons.
You cannot own what you cannot walk to.
And Juanita's sky?
An extension of the storms within?
Is that where we find songs
ageless or simply old?
Germán seems to read my thoughts:
And then there was Dímela (tell it to me). People
would call out to him "dímela," and he would look
at his right sole and tell them the exact time.
I wonder if it's too late to be Cuban.
Around three in the morning we go to Versailles for café
and Germán tells me, Right here not too long ago
I was waiting my turn when a man with a scar
on his face came up to another man drinking his cafecito.
The scarred man looked the other man in the eye
and asked, Don't you recognize me? Look again,
are you sure you don't recognize this face?
You gave me this scar in an acto de repudio
during Mariel. What are you doing in Miami now?
The fists of the scarred man fell upon the former

communist and nearly killed him. The cops came.
Those old songs remind me of the actos de repudio,
says Germán, the mobs of communists clubbing people
who simply presented their papers to leave the country.
I saw a pregnant woman, bludgeoned, giving birth
right on the street. And a fifteen-year-old girl,
torn from her parents and chased to the bridge
over the Guaso River. They stripped her
and hung her by her ankles over the river.
I knew her family, Ricardo.
Later, in exile, she would kill herself.
What do you get from those songs, Ricardo?
Dímelo. What do you get from those songs?

Years of Exile

RICARDO PAU-LLOSA
— After the paintings of Humberto Calzada

The water enters the old ballroom
and the once bedroom, seeps across
the erstwhile chessboard floor
where rumors made their way.
The squares once mapped
the tinted flights of sun
that stained-glass half-wheels wrote,
pages in the metronome diary of an age.
These testaments only seemed random,
stretched lights falling like
premeditated leaves
against the staring wall
or upon the lurid waist of the piano.

And then the water came.
The first arrival left
a pale ghost on the tiles.
Later more water came and more
so that no one could show
the uninvited flood the door,
which was half drowned.
The glass wheels turned
their voices on the murk.

And we waited for the new day
when losses would turn to stories.
We would laugh, we knew it, about
the swallowed rooms, the stabbed
recollections where gilded curtains
and danzones swayed.

But the years knew better.
We have learned to love
the cracks on the ceiling,
a nose away. We stare into them now
that we have learned to float and have become
the Sistine chroniclers of our shrinkings.
We create, we are free
now that we have lost count of everything.

California

PAUL HOOVER

From the cool electric gaze of a Hollywood enigma
to the cormorant eating fish at a Muir Beach tide pool,
the state's a deep oasis of appetite and ease.
The newspaper reports eighty quakes a week,
most of them temblors faint as a star on water.
As whole hands of fog drape over the Golden Gate,
a piano in Oakland moans like a choir.
In the High Sierras, falling snow
is blue as brand-new skin;
the world's weight is measured
by a metaphysical Reno as clean as Disneyland.
Closer to Sacramento, the hum of BMWs
on their way to a software convention
sounds tasteful in the rain.
The motel owner knows the desert speed
of screenplays, since he is writing one
in the neon light of a nude but lucid room.
A postmodern bar just opened down the street.
No dancing, no smoking, no alcohol are allowed.
But you can get a mud bath, scented body wrap,
and whales hysterically singing
directly into your headphones.
The county sheriff has a Ph.D. and surfs the Internet.
Relations are wreathed with chaos theory
and the "new world order."
    As the millennium approaches and nature
politely recedes, everyone thinks good thoughts.
Former cheerleaders join a woman's drumming circle.
The family leaves the Methodist Church
for a sweat lodge in the country. In the absence
of the Soviet Union, Satan makes a comeback

along with angels who look like airline stewards,
cheeks rosy with steroids and purpose.
But they're on leave or out of work.
Narcissus drowns in a tide pool while reflecting
on a starfish; Sisyphus rides a mountain bike
up Mt. Tamalpais, where Zeus confuses omniscience
with his remote control. The future oversleeps.
But in a trailer home in Rancho Cucamonga,
the present has a theory scratched as paradise.
Bruise's star is dark.

    The bargain was to sing, as populations do,
the terrors of pleasure, like holding the gecko's tail
after it has dropped. Disguised by rear-view worlds,
we have taken steps in just that direction.
Glad the puritans came, we wander back repressed
to the land we would unsettle. Darkness
swallows borders. A wilderness shines.

Still Kicking in America

G. S. SHARAT CHANDRA

Nothing changes in America
for Asians who write in English.
Now that I'm older,
the old ones ask
the same questions
the young ones asked
when I was younger.
Where did you learn such good English?
A Polish wife of a travelling professor
dangles her earrings vehemently,
lifts the hem of her dainty skirt
to show me thighs that withstood
long lines, dictators,
before she kicked them for good.

Kicking a country
with such strong legs
is some kind of victory.
I look at my own
vegetarian calves,
so starved and tubular
even Gandhi would be ashamed.
But these are calves
that never kicked anyone
but their owner
in dreams or desperation,
hoping for words
to come out right in English.

Persona

BRIGITTE BYRD

I suddenly feel Slav, oh, no, not suave, rather Slavic. You know,
lyrical, melancholy, mesmerized by wailing Tzigane melodies' stroke

on distant violins and broken voices that sing strange stories
I do not comprehend, laments of wanderers descended from Adam

and his first, mysterious wife, not Eve, or from a handful of enigmatic
Atlantes. What if these mournful cries come from Roms crammed

in dreary housing developments scattered on the outskirts
of cities like weeds worn by mourners to remind us of our fate?

What if this language spoken by the elders around a forbidden fire
desperately tries to revive fading memories of the old nomadic ways

buried under a forced, aimless sedentary life? A language approaching death.
Oh, what else but my voluntary isolation or maybe the ambiguous juxtaposition

of great expectations for my new language with the insidious loss
of my *langue* could cause this nostalgia for the East I once visited

and left with relief because seeds sprouted between eroded cobblestones
and bleak, empty grocery shelves kept reflecting a chaotic world

I came to entertain at the Budapest State Circus. Joy. Remembrance
of a word after seconds of hesitation and fear of losing my language, my culture.

Delusion. I never wore the *diklo*, the green and red scarf of the married woman.
My waist and my shoulders have no memory of the sash, and my heavy, glittering

jewelry does not show my wealth but sparkles in the spotlights to attract
the audience's attention on my painted eyes, half-naked breast, and hidden sex.

Instead of eloping with a dark lover, surrendering to his fiery eyes
and to my lot, I choose to make my fortune and roam the world

on my own. I travel in the luxurious confinement of an embellished wagon
of the Orient Express. Paris, Vienna, the Magyar plains, Keleti Station.

I join the *Gens du voyage* for the winter months, meet the Bougliones's son
and his *fauves*, a tantalizing Frederick-Fredericka, an army of aged contortionists,

a sad clown. I find myself among a flock of chorus girls striving to avoid
a gigantic silver ball preceding the lion's exit, before we make our magnificent

entrance dressed like birds of Paradise. Awakening. Back in my comfortable
nest perched on the sixth floor of *Avenue des Ternes*, I looked westwards

toward the New World, ready to create my new persona and give a fatal blow
to the old rich uncle stories. I am *la tante d'Amerique* who builds up a stock of words.

Farragut North

STANLEY PLUMLY

In the tunnel-light at the top of the station two or three
figures huddled under tarps built against the wind crossing
Connecticut at K. It'll be noon before they rise in their
Navajo blankets, trinkets, ski masks and gloves to start
the day, noon before the oil slicks of ice on the sidewalks thaw. —
In the forties, after the war, in the Land of Uz, when
somebody came to the house for a handout, my mother'd give
him milk money or bread money as well as bread and milk.
To her each day was the thirties. The men at the door had
the hard-boiled faces of veterans, soldiers of the enemy.
My mother saw something in them, homelessness the condition
of some happiness, as if in the faces of these drifters could be
read pieces of parts of herself still missing: like the Indian
woman in Whitman's *Sleepers* who comes to his mother's door
looking for work when there is no work yet is set by the fire
and fed: so that for my mother, the first time she left,
it became a question of whom to identify with most,
the wanderer or the welcomer. — The stunted sycamores on K are
terminal, though they'll outlast the hairline fractures marbling
the gravestones of the buildings. Under the perfect pavement
of the sky the figures frozen in this landscape contemplate
the verities too fundamentally for city or country: their isolation
is complete, like the dead or gods. When I think of a day with
nothing in it, a string of such days, I think of the gray life of
buildings, of walking out of my life in a direction just
invented, or, since some of us survive within the mental wards
of our own third worlds, I see myself disguised for constant
winter, withdrawn into the inability to act on the least impulse
save anger and hear myself in street-talk talking street-time.
— Such is the freedom of transformation, letting the deep
voice climb on its own; such is the shell of the body broken,
falling away like money's new clothes; such is my mother's
truant spirit, moving dead leaves with the wind among the shadows. . . .

In the Twilight Zone All I Know Is the Commercials

PATRICIA GOEDICKE

Big things in the wind:
Big dirty things in the wind.

All across America is that our underwear
Flapping on the clotheslines are those our mangy sheets

Well I'd like to know whose they are

Gleaming like Abraham Lincoln's spectacles
Are those my false teeth

Is that Thomas Jefferson's flying heartache
Do those moth-eaten buffalo belong to me

Well I'd like to know whose they are

Rolling around above me like a baseball
Is that my Babe Ruth, is that my President
Eavesdropping on the other team's plays,

Is that my scandal with the sincere hair and the baby blue eyes,
Is that my True Confessions, my tape recorder, my homemade bomb,

Well I'd like to know whose they are

If I'm committing the sin of pride please stop me,
I mean I'm a responsible citizen

Every four years I vote but I can't help it,
Who can predict what will happen
In the Twilight Zone all I know is the commercials,

But if those aren't my Congressmen or my Senators
If those aren't my brown babies

If those aren't my Jews
Expelled again, from the new Eden

Getting into the same old cattlecars, and wailing
like tattered black birds across the heavens

Well I'd like to know whose they are

Dust and Broughtonia

RANDALL MANN

And I, wishing to be back in Cuba,
wandered a room rich with rocking chairs.
Alone on the nightstand,

The Count of Monte Cristo, bound in leather
and dust. Dust the window.
I smudged the panes with my right cuff:

greenhouses of madder crimson Broughtonia;
barbed fences dripping with bougainvillea;
wild flowers by the roadside, deeper than dye —

but I saw only Broughtonia,
purple cousins of these displaced red ones,
purpling only the mountains of Cuba.

Two Sounds

MICHAEL BUGEJA

— for my son

Grandmother came here in the cargo hold
Of a great vessel and loved the tap of rain
On roofs, the ocean ever in her ears,
Grooved cornucopias that echo still
In this empty shell like a wavelength.
Can you hear the soothing *rattle-tap-tap*
Gutter-drip, her fingertip on your pane?
You, too, will lose and find me in this hymn

At 40, dreading another dawn. Listen
Then to the arias of robin and starling
Grandmother fed with bread I did not eat
On her lawn, happy to wake to the warbling,
As we wait now, sleepless but together.
I have loaned you these legacies of sound
To outlast the apparitions of light
Which always fade, as I will, in the night.

Under the Freeway in El Paso

RAY GONZALEZ

I hear streets light up
with secret weeping,

wish I could really hear it,
be given the owl

and the route of veins
pulsing under the freeway

where the house of my birth
stands and decays.

Strangers have lived there
for the last thirty-eight years.

I have wanted to knock on the door
and breathe inside the house.

Someone wants me
to disguise myself as a street,

a traffic signal or a dark alley,
the imploded house across

from the last residence
of the ghost who follows me inside.

Someone wants me to thrive,
surpass the disappearance

of my father, my dead grandfathers,
my missing uncle, my cousins

who won't speak to me because
I come from the house of candles,

the room of saints, the wall of glowing
crucifixes that break the arms

of those who don't believe,
who curse the smoke

and blow it toward me,
the blankets I found inside

shattered rooms under
the freshly built freeway.

I went crazy with hope there,
restless as the prisoner

who fell down the hill,
impaled himself on yucca

and the turnpike of America,
the pointed staff of the priest.

I am the man who ate
the catacombs of honey,

raised my lips to the wiping hands
that took care of me inside the house,

gave me sweetness of prayer,
the stranger waiting for my return,

so he could light the candles
that didn't melt in the years of the passenger.

Todorov at Ellis Island

MAXINE CHERNOFF

The secret of narrative
in the sight of the lovely
original fixtures,
the false accusations,
"K" for insanity.
An indigent writer,
specifying the predicate,
fear of fire in ramshackle
buildings, the ghost
of the fantastic looking
across frozen water.
He felt swallowed up
by the 200 stairs,
by a procedure based on
external criteria,
plot and genre likely
to become a public charge.
While from the mountains
of Northern Italy, refused
admittance, a girl acting
mad, alluding to hermits
and saints. For to destroy
does not mean to ignore,
does not mean to build
the story-machine nor to feel
the grass under foot, but
to turn, as if spoken to,
into what we represent.

Dixie

Now if you want to drive 'way sorrow,
Come and hear dis song to-morrow.
— Daniel Decatur Emmett

— for Bob Cantwell

I.
I had no idea.
In Ohio, in a field
near where we've found ourselves
black-hearted and alone,
where the winter-blanched
stalks or corn stubble stand around,
wind rasping through

their ripped sleeves, where
yesterday the whole field seemed
a sad, gray blur
after last week's scum of snow,
the Snowden brothers' twin stones
crumbled and are gone.
Proud relatives, you guessed,

or some high-minded public
servant, must have remembered
the two sons of slaves
just long enough to engrave
and raise one more,
store-bought stone, there
in the backwoods churchyard

where we marched
over the grave-soft earth.
Weak light fell
through the frames of black branches
where no song was.
Only: *They Taught Dixie*
To Dan Emmett.

2.
Braced by snow, but booted hard,
the back door for days locked
tight with ice gave way.
And so help us both, we tramped into
no good single story again, your home.
The logs we lugged in,
the weeping logs we stacked and lit

could barely thaw each other out
to burn. The walls glowed
with their other life, your daughters'
drawings plastered everywhere:
dazzling suns, ruby trees, birds colored
every possibility, summer pictures
like sweet outflung windows

the cruel wind blew into,
frameless as mirrors, back-looking, devastating,
beautiful. Our guitars loved us
the little they could,
two freezing singers whose lives
slept safely somewhere else,
in the concurrent dark,

whose songs were stolen.
Isn't that the irony
of displacement, that we remember ourselves
through others? The whiskey's smolder
faded late and slow. Outside
the sleet crept scraping
among the haggard trees, like a spy.

3.

Uncle Dan in blackface,
Uncle Dan in greatcoat and boots stomping
across the stage-planks, deliberate
in his dirge, a walk-around so pure
with longing and regrets
the audience shuts up and stares:
In Dixie's Land where I was born

Early on one frosty morn,
Look a-way . . . up-state New York, 1859.
It's snowing, how many hundreds
of miles from Ohio
where the Snowden brothers pluck banjos
and sing for passing coaches
from their porch. He's on his way

to being famous, his minstrels
in demand, though today his white ears
crack in ferocious cold. He turns,
spanks and twists his floured hands
high in the air, though
his back seems broken
it's so bent, and now shuffles

to the other side, face colored
into a negative of clown,
singing of mistakes . . . *Look a-way,*
Dixie's Land. Camera powder explodes
and clapping scares a flock
of pigeons from their oak. He watches them
scatter, recollect, fly away.

4.
Snow falls over Ohio.
I have a window so wide
it's like I'm sitting outside, easy chair
kicked back, half-drunk, freezing.
The truth is, I've been trying to write
a love poem all this time
and don't know how. She's gone

and won't come back, next-door neighbor
to your daughters in that fenced-off,
foreign country inside this one.
If I sight them right, along
my thumb, the stumps align
like crumbled, nameless, blackened stones
in a graveyard — but you know that

already. The trees
crowd around gray in their daguerreotype.
It should be spring but snow keeps coming.
There should be flowers
but the stubble field and fencerows
grow only murderous with crows.
Like little pieces

of a poem gone wrong, and torn,
the snow keeps floating down,
and she is gone.
Uncle Dan lived a long time
and I have his words on good authority:
I wish I had never writ
that God-damn song.

5.
How do you tell people
you love them in this cold
country too big for its own good?
So help me, I can't stop
from seeing the children, blood-wild
and eager, trooping across
their families' fields,

the stolen song of another country
gone wrong on their lips.
I can't stop from seeing
the Snowdens starving for a song.
I had no idea
it would turn out like this.
Like some silly, lovely-painted clown,

a bluejay fiddles away right now
in the redbud's heart,
harping on and on outside
my picture window. I look away.
You would say he's full of life, old friend,
and you'd be right. You would say,
in all your hope and sadnesses,

he signals the going-on of things.
And you'd be right again, I'm almost afraid
to think. I see you sitting
in your summer-frozen house, alone,
thumbing a book, breathing into your hands,
and wish the same old wish, that we were
anywhere but here.

The Extinct Homeland —
A Conversation with Czeslaw Milosz

ANA DOINA

Tell me, as you would in the middle of the night
When we face only night, the ticking of a watch,
The whistle of an express train, tell me
Whether you really think that this world
Is your home?
— *"An Appeal" by Czeslaw Milosz*

Home? Somewhere we belong? The metaphor
which includes us in its landscape? The place
that always takes us in, gives us context
is part of our texture? A land where, no matter
how scorched the soil, our roots can still grow?
Where all that we should, could, would have been
realized? There is no home for us, Czeslaw.
There is no homeland. Not anymore, not anywhere.

I wish I could learn to live with the malady
of an elsewhere, with the "hidden certainty"
that trees grow taller, and sunset's peacock tail
opens more intense colors over other horizons, or else
quit trying to understand here in comparison with there
as if I never am where I am, as if I never embody
my own presence.

I wish I could cease to crave a pathway
to a physical place I come from, or go to,
and like nomads who don't know where
they have started their exile, I could accept
oblivion as enough of a homeland.

Czeslaw, you've been at this game
far longer than I, tell me, is elsewhere real?
Or did I create a lucid paradise of what exists
only in memory? Obsessive, like the negative
of an otherwise ordinary picture. Do I,
haunted by the need for symmetry — a known beginning
to a perceivable end — hold real what I choose to keep
alive and harmonious through my story? Do I,
asking for the benefit of nostalgia — this hallucination
whose life is hunger and thirst — break bread
with a Fata Morgana?

Homeland — its cannibal mouth, open
like a graveyard, threatened to swallow me. I too
ran away from my civilization foolishly thinking
I would be able to escape it, and emerge
from the narrow cocoon of my flight like a butterfly
who has no memory of the caterpillar. But no land
lets itself be eradicated without leaving behind ruins
or fossils. And no new ground is comparable
to what becomes sweeter through memory. Homeland —
inscrutable, freed from its bitterness, turns into a garden
while the present, always a temporary ark, is no salvation,
only a journey without a known destination.

I must have been kneaded out of a clay that doesn't stick
to the potter's hands and is not one with the rest of the earth,
and just like wisdom words don't keep the breath of the wise,
my life once undone from its originating landscape cannot
be tied to a place anymore. Nor to the sword-laden history
whose blood throbs in my temples, nor to an ancestral oath
which still awakens forgotten passions when I bite
the bitter bread of a past ethnic pride. Not even to a generic
alley between columnar poplars. All I have are images
voices, faces of people and angels — memorized.

A homeland that neither lives, nor dies, but stays
crystallized like a picture.

All there is is a harsh saddle I haven't yet broken in
and the promise of a mythology that doesn't remember
people trudging out of burning pasts, a mythology
that doesn't describe fog-encircled forests and rolling hills,
but a calling, a thirst.

Exiled I make a vow to be what I don't know
to a land I haven't inherited, while the old homeland,
the one that becomes extinct in the distance, survives
only in my mouth, in the flavors I long for,
in the mother tongue I teach to my children.

There is no homeland. I am its preexisting condition.
I am the great-grandmother of someone who will not
remember the exact place I came from, or why
I needed to run away from the ancestral land, or how
I worshiped. I am my own myth, the first memory, nebulous
like any beginning.

13th Arrondissement Blues

BARBARA HAMBY

When we sit down for yet another sublime meal
    at Quán Huê on the Avenue de Choisy, instead of the usual
Vietnamese hit parade, a tape of Beatles tunes erupts
    in the quiet room, not covers, but the Fab Four
themselves belting out their watered down rockabilly hits,
    beginning with "Ticket to Ride," and all the ultra-chic
French in the restaurant start swaying back and forth
    as if hypnotized by some pop culture Svengali, singing
in ridiculous English, "She's gotta teeket to ri-i-i-ide,"
    even the sad-looking woman and her bored husband wailing
like John Lennon, and when I order my *rouleau de printemps*,
    the waiter is singing, "She woz a daytripper,
one-way ticket, yeah," and I figure he was about minus
    15 years old when that came out and his parents,
if they'd even met each other much less thought of him,
    were dodging bombs my ex-schoolmates and my father's
colleagues were dropping on their homeland, and when he delivers
    my beer the whole restaurant is singing "Roll Over
Beethoven," conjuring the shadow of those teenaged toughs
    in Liverpool listening to scratchy LPs of old Delta
bluesmen, their pommaded scions, the anarchy of Little Richard,
    luminous misery of B. B. King, Robert Johnson's tawny grief,
down as any human being could be and as I eat my bowl
    of *vermicelles avec porc grillé au citrónelle*, the tape
loops back to John Lennon wailing, haranguing the dark slave
    of love in the heart of everyone, naked, chained by impulses
we can hardly control, trying to understand why our hearts
    are breaking like a ship off the stony coast of some unknown
new world, a thunderous storm breaking the masts,
    the crew washed overboard, the captain impaled

on the rigging, misery and greed swept into the vast maw
    of the hungry ocean, and we're in the churning water,
unchained at last, falling down waves steep as mountains,
    drinking salt as if it were wine, the sun breaking
through purple clouds, in the distance a fingernail of sand,
    and if only we could swim, we might be free.

La Lupe

VICTOR HERNÁNDEZ CRUZ

Her voice comes out of her knees,
her fingernails are full of sound,
birds are in her lungs,
which gives her gargantual flight,
a fluorescence through ether waves,
like ancestral Morse codes.

Santiago de Cuba
her first steps.
At nineteen she dismantled retinas —
roosters blew themselves inside out,
when she swayed by cathedrals they folded,
guayacan trees fell to their knees,
mountains bowed with the contents of ajiaco.
She filled the horizon with kerchiefs,
gypsies dancing behind her,
her bracelets were snakes.
Forces were captured in her gold chains,
the moon was in her silver.
There were reptiles stationed
in her Afro-Siboney cheeks,
there was in her Asian eyes
radar picking up the fingertips
of the piano player —
the language of the trumpet —
black changos landing upon
the shelf of her eyelids.

She motioned in songs to live them.
Her passion destroyed the container,
she blew up into false promises,

romantic lyrics tied her in knots,
broken into pieces of kisses.
She knew it was "theater" that
which you offered,
a landscape hanging in the
museums of desire,
rows of guayaba paste,
stones all according
to your point of view,
salons of dried roses.
Illusions.

Her songs became the windows
of the city,
in the distance a hurt bellows
from a bird locked in a radio.

Classroom teacher of tropical children,
reading to them native flora —
a wind entered her and she flew to
New York,
eating the skyline,
bridges of electric lights,
conduits to the house of the Saints.
At the Jefferson Theater
she melted the microphone
into liquid mercury,
and an ambulance had to
get her off the stage.

She embodied in gowns, capes,
dresses, necklaces, bonnets,
velvets, suedes, diamond studded,
flowers, sequins,
all through which

she wanted to eat herself.
She savaged us all,
but took the radiation.
Each time she sang
she crossed the sea.
From the Bronx
she went back to Cuba,
adrift on the sails
of a song.

Rafael Hernández

VICTOR HERNÁNDEZ CRUZ

Born exactly in Aguadilla
north coast Puerto Rico —
a stellar light of such aim
focused among the wooden houses —
how the wind cooperates
lifting the skirts
of Atlantean seashells resounding
like bells made of glass,
Rafael saw each tree twice
the same way a woman
walks her eyes
sharp charcoal becomes light —

Island beauty like the poets
of sight who could paint
with words —
saw the mountains the way
they saw themselves
Creators eyes —
it was not by chance
the space of his birth
pin-pointed the tropical night —
composer of sound
songs with the people
in which the whole landscape
cinemas through the lips,
when he left for other lands,
he took the trees with him,
put rivers in his pockets,
condensed amapolas into his pores,
he'd be sitting in Harlem

listening to Carib frogs.
Congolese rhythms would
come to his guarachas,
cachitas of his youth
danced for him in Mexico,
they scaled the pyramid walls
dancing plenas and bombas,
on 166th Street
he saw an ox pushing a carriage
with a load of sweet cane.

The popular follows the people
and consequently the people
follow the popular
they become one with the air.

Rafael wore his hats
like a poetic meter
to achieve decimas
to do rag-time
with Jim Europe band
Viva Paris.

What sings in the Americas
passes through his filters,
all impossible love
an odyssey yearning to touch,
dreaming awake.

This illusive girl
that is a gesture in a mirror
each limerick points on the map —
of her possible location,
ask Dante or Cervantes
this is what makes the road —

what builds cities,
Rafael with his load
with his joy
left towards civilization,
full of a place without legislation
with only the creature's body
a green mineral
floating upon blue liquid
beautiful without insignias
a pebble of mother earth
a womb
a nation
becoming in his words
giving birth
to the children of
eternal liberation.

To Be Sung on the Fourth of July

WYATT PRUNTY

We come to this country
By every roundabout,
With hunger like a startled face
And passports folding doubt,

With leaving home as commonplace
As children waking clear,
And hopeful as a fishline cast
Deep from the harbor's pier

To the idea of a country,
The garden and the name,
And a government by language,
Called the New Jerusalem,

Where the trees have figured upward
As much as shadowed down;
And when we stood beneath them
We hugely looked around,

Because our gift is figures
That turn along our thought,
The apple, rock, and water,
The ram suddenly caught —

A country of inheritors
Who only learn of late,
Who set their eyes as blankly
As their livestock stand and wait,

There where the markets bicker
Till the bell has rung them home,
There where Chicago bargains
The wheat crop for a loan,

Wait like the black lake barges
That punctuate a course
Or linger in ellipsis
Between the yawning shores . . .

And then that huge interior
That always seems the same,
Abandoned wells, neglected fields,
And immigrants who came

Mapping the land they traveled for,
Stayed, worked a while, then died,
Or moved to cities where
They also worked and died

As, settlers who burned and built
And surveyed every line,
We timbered, plowed, and harvested
To songs in three-four time.

Our figures are like fireworks,
And water turned to fire;
In Cleveland or Chicago
The people never tire

Of the ballads of an innocence
That would not be dissolved,
But burned the witch and stuck like tar . . .
To the first citizen ever saved.

And though at times in chorus,
The music almost right,
We sing away the darkness
That makes a window bright,

In fact we're born too lucky
To see a street's neglect,
For the years have pushed us next to
An unalike Elect —

Who say the lost are with us
The way our backs go bad
Or eyes require new glasses
To peer into what's sad,

Which occupies the TV set
And functions by contrast,
Because well-being needs a grief
To make the feeling last.

New York Public Library

SUSAN THOMAS

Five young men get off the boat in New York City.
It is 1909. They are students from Vilna.
They go to the New York Public Library.
They can't believe their eyes.
So many books, such long tables!
And the lamps! The comfort of the chairs!
Day after day they go to the library.
Each one studies what is closest to his heart.

At closing time they go for rolls and coffee.
They discuss what each has learned;
twenty years old, they know
this can't go on forever.
Soon they must get jobs, raise families.
One of them has an idea.
He will figure out what two things
Americans buy the most. Then he
will combine them into one thing.
What could be simpler?
He will start the business
make a big success
become a millionaire
and hire someone else to run things
while he studies in the library.

The other young men get jobs.
They are working long hours now
in offices and factories.
Only one is still at the library.
He studies every day
the reports of what Americans buy.

It seems chocolate is popular
and also laxatives. Why not,
he thinks, a chocolate laxative?
Americans can enjoy themselves
while they take a physic.
Soon nobody even says laxative
anymore. Now they say Ex-lax.
The young man returns
to the library, where he studies
astronomy and insects.

Public School No. 18, Paterson, New Jersey

MARIA MAZZIOTTI GILLAN

Miss Wilson's eyes, opaque
as blue glass, fix on me:
"We must speak English.
We're in America now."
I want to say, "I am American,"
but the evidence is stacked against me.

My mother scrubs my scalp raw, wraps
my shining hair in white rags
to make it curl. Miss Wilson
drags me to the window, checks my hair
for lice. My face wants to hide.

At home, my words smooth in my mouth,
I chatter and am proud. In school,
I am silent, grope for the right English
words, fear the Italian word
will sprout from my mouth like a rose,

fear the progression of teachers
in their sprigged dresses,
their Anglo-Saxon faces.

Without words, they tell me
to be ashamed.
I am.
I deny that booted country
even from myself,
want to be still
and untouchable
as these women
who teach me to hate myself.

Years later, in a white
Kansas City house,
the Psychology professor tells me
I remind him of the Mafia leader
on the cover of *Time* magazine.

My anger spits
venomous from my mouth:

I am proud of my mother,
dressed all in black,

proud of my father
with his broken tongue,
proud of the laughter
and noise of our house.

Remember me, Ladies,
the silent one?
I have found my voice
and my rage will blow
your house down.

Whereabouts

ROBERT PHILLIPS
— *for Richard Howard*

Isn't it odd how anyone who disappeared
      is said to have been sighted in San Francisco?
What is it about that city with its steep
      streets that so inclines them?

Consider Judge Crater, snapped by Polaroid
      weeding on his knees in his San Mateo garden.
Or the Brach candy heiress after a quake,
      stuffing currency into a sidewalk crevice,

generous to a fault. Ambrose Bierce is seen
      and heard rehearsing his *Devil's Dictionary*
in a Chinese take-out joint on Grant.
      And that boy with bangs pushing crack

and his buns in Haight-Ashbury? Etan Patz,
      no longer young, eyes cunning and feral.
Jimmy Hoffa, set deep in the cement
      of his ways, emerges from the Sheraton-Palace,

a floozie on each arm. He's come a long way
      from Detroit. And wasn't that Amelia Earhart
boarding the Red Eye at International,
      wearing only one size-9 Cat's Paw shoe?

There's Dick Diver strap-hanging on a cable car,
      Michael Rockefeller atop the Transamerica,
Weldon Kees still contemplating San Francisco Bay,
      '52 Ford on the approach ramp. He never left.

Don't they know we need them all to stay away?
>Our mythology's poor enough even without them.
They must remain precisely as last seen,
>just before fadeout, their famous last scene.

Reading Kerouac, Yorkshire

STEVE WILSON

1.   Today, Jack, your words won't console
me. They've sent me stumbling along
through my own past. At the edge of what
I am, I'm bent for a path near the river
below Rievaulx Abbey — sound

of my steps through grass. The abbey
stones are thick and brittle — old
pages where monks tried
their silences, gone wild now
like Italian flowers. Reading you,

I've drifted centuries out,
among decay. We learn —
to be alone is to open ourselves to
trees hard against the hills,
light on water.

2.   It's night, and be sure,
you are still no friend of mine, memory.
When I look beyond you to the river

in its turning flow, I think I might
fall into a deep bowl of sleep, slip over to
the side of the wind we never see. Disappear.

What will the darkness leave
of me? Black trees, then nothing
but the dark. Lovers gone. We are

the faint lines in a leaf, you and I.
No friends in the world but the thirst
we would taste in our minds.

—summer 1997

King of Wounds

SEAN BRENDAN-BROWN

He lived on our place
since before I was born —
more uncle than hired hand.
Pawnee, he changed his name
to King of Wounds after Korea
part joke, part serious

because he believed fighting
the Chinese had changed
his vision forever at Chosin:
the vision he had at fourteen
of an owl flying loop-the-loops
in a circle of red moon, talons
clutching a shrieking white
rabbit. His name then had been
Johnny No-Horses. He returned
from Korea with a box of medals
and as scarred as Frankenstein but enough
disability pension it didn't matter no
one was hiring Indians;
my father hired him.

King of Wounds. Odd even among
men reluctant to judge. He rode his
circuit of fence at night because that's
when cattle break out or men in.
He loved stars and meteor showers
and considered insomnia a blessing.
A beautiful woman once tried to lure
him to the city — she tried everything.
They had a good time and King of Wounds

wore the pearl button shirts she bought
but at last she went home alone.
When I asked him about it all he said was
> on those barren islands
> they die blamed and blaming.

Easter, Circa 1960

PETER JOHNSON

Such a clattering of black shoes. Mine are very tight and have pointed toes. "Spic shoes," my father calls them, which is fine with me, as I fashion my pompadour and place a gangster-style hat on my head. My cheeks are fat, my pants tight around the ass. A boy was stabbed yesterday. I stood with the older boys and watched, the arc of the knife's blade like a silver fish rising for water spiders. The kitchen table glows with bowls of shrimp and hot cocktail sauce. A giant urn of potato chips gives shape to the living room. After dinner, my father argues with my grandparents, and everyone goes home. I take the chips to my room. Lie down. Click my Cuban heels.

Salt Longing

AUSTIN HUMMELL

Inland far though and away
from the cursive coast that bore us
under smaller village roofs,
where the rain was stranger to the earth
than our voices to the sea.

Farther than the gratitude
of hands that touch us or don't,
no landlocked drawl reaches
deltas into our salt birth.

What state can hide the sea like this,
in sharkless gardens and midwest rain?
The owls are not what they seem
beneath their nervous rhetoric,
and the quail speak their own names.

Where in this land split
by the river of big canoes
is the blowsy shade of willows,
the oak hammocks where ferns and ivy lie?

Maybe I'm lost in a stand of loblollies
and Missouri is a sugared dream.
Maybe I'm thirty in a coil of banyans
dipping limbs into origins like Florida —

its spongy, sinking soil —
its scorched, ashen soil.

History Class

TINO VILLANUEVA

— Clase de historia, *translated by James Hoggard*

To enter was to breathe in
the illegitimate idea of the class:
only what was written was valid.
Seated in the same
prescribed place
I felt myself, finally, dislocated.
I looked all around
and nothing was shining for me.

It was some morning in autumn,
or the spring of '59, and already we were
the wheat-colored people
who felt alien,
as if no one would intercede for us,
because to enter was to defy
the suffocating results
of the conflict: the state against us with no weapon
of a retrievable date
to wield
against the long speeches
of that teacher
with the hard Southern mien,
creator of the dream and hierarchies,
who repeated,
as if it were his mission,
my people's crippled history:

And beware of the Mexicans, when
they press you to hot coffee and
"tortillas." Put fresh caps on
your revolver, and see that your

"shooting-irons" are all in order,
for you will probably need them
before long. They are a great
deal more treacherous than Indians.

That corrupt teacher was not
among the authors of the light,
nor did he help
the quick brains of my people grow
with his facile remarks
and snobbish attitude:

He will feed you on his best,
"señor" you, and "muchas gracias"
you, and bow to you like a French
dancing-master, and wind it all up
by slipping a knife under your
left shoulder blade! And that's
one reason I hate them so.

To keep from crying out the anger boiling up in me
I bent over my desk
like a human question mark;
I imagined myself in another state,
but I was falling
each time toward humiliation's
dense abyss,
the persistent theme of my time.
Who were we
other than some kids
detained at the perverse border
of prejudice, still without
effective documents
to proclaim our freedom?
My tongue went crazy.

I wanted to know right away
and to say something to stop
the abecedarian of power,
to lift myself up and with one blow
split the enemy's
obsessive phrases, and let loose
arguments about our courage
and plant, in the middle of class,
the badge of my faith.
But all was silence,
obedience to the infected
dark cast of the texts,
and it was too early
during that morning in autumn
or spring of '59
to say
what needed to be said.

But the years passed
and the books changed
to the beat of the people's rhythm,
because only for a while
can a man
carry on his back
the burden
of the one who thinks he's a conqueror.

Here my life scars over
because I'm the deserter,
the profane impenitent who quit
the crazy class,
the insurrectionist
stripped of the creeds of negation.

So let there be
other words that are triumphant
and not the ones of infamy,
those of the blinding fraud.

Death of a War Hero

MICHAEL BUGEJA

— *for Emmanuel A. (1919–94)*

So many Rambo movies have been made
It's hard to consider a war hero
Being anything other than Anglo
Or dumb as Forrest Gump playing ping-pong
In the MIA alleys of Haiphong.

My immigrant uncle was brown and meek.
When he cried, rivulets would map his cheek
Like swollen tributaries of the Rhine.
Someone issued him an MI carbine
And he used it. He resembled a rookie

Sensation for the legendary Yankees —
Yogi Berra — which was something back then.
He lived in the shadow of that icon,
Squat as a catcher with a different mask:
Death. The grim reaper is not as grotesque

As you think. Say "Emmanuel" to it.
Once he entrapped an entire unit
In the bloody Ardennes and ambushed them
With other assassins. The stratagem
Worked. By nightfall, the Nazi field marshal

Had lost a dozen men and his morale,
Lower than the Führer in his bunker.
The Wehrmacht was routed. He could suffer
This tiny defeat, hoisting a hankie
And waving the way fans do at Yankee

Stadium when a rookie points his bat.
Emmanuel pointed a bayonet
At the enemy and told them to drop
Their rifles in a pile. The sniping stopped.
The Americans emerged from the woods.

Again my uncle had beaten the odds
And encircled a field marshal with a *von*
In between his names, a blueblood Saxon
Analyzing another rabble of "Yanks"
And bearing a sidearm with ruby and onyx

Swastikas on the handle. My uncle stepped
Forward with those sorry cheeks. He had wept
Because he slew Aryan boys littler
Than he who were wearing the same Hitler
Insignia on infantry uniforms

Instead of pinstripes. He noted the sidearm.
The field marshal noted the rifle-pile,
Wanting to fight again. He could reconcile
His capture, it seemed, but not his captor,
Daring Emmanuel to massacre

Prisoners or permit them to retake
Positions. The German made a mistake,
As if this was the end of an inning,
Not a battle, with my uncle brandishing
A bat and not a bayonet. He looked up.

He was always looking up in the hope
Those looking down would see beyond the mask.
"What gives you the right?" the German asked
In the flawless American lingo
Nazis learned along with "DiMaggio"

And "Berra." My uncle hated baseball.
He aimed and unloaded a bullet-hail,
Winging the officer's bluebloody head.
"This gives me the right," Emmanuel said
In a language everyone understood.

Later that year outside Weimar he would
Help free Buchenwald. The inmates amassed
Along the barbwire fence as he passed
To open the gate. They stood eye-level
And saw death incarnate. They knew it well,

And the name "Emmanuel" meant nothing.
Substitute father, he meant everything
To me growing up in the stadium-shadow.
Yogi Berra was back, hawking "Yoo-hoo"
In a bowling alley off U.S. 3.

My uncle suffered a half century
What we call Post-Traumatic Stress Syndrome.
The holocaust was real in our home.
"Each life you took," I told him, "you gave back
Liberating that camp." He wouldn't talk.

Words were meaningless. But they could still haunt.
Emmanuel died at a restaurant
Without help of the Heimlich maneuver,
Something the enemy pulls in a war.
Finally the paramedics arrived

Encircling him, managing to revive
A heart beat by jump-starting the body
As mechanics do a car battery,
Attaching the electrical cables.
Emmanuel had left the vehicle

Of life idling there by accident,
Tethered to tubes in a hospital tent.
Soon his fingers curled as if in anger
Trying to grasp invisible triggers
In that room. Doctors cut intravenous

And no one in the name of Christ Jesus
Picketed that decision. He was just
Another survivor going to waste
Without food and water, the iron gate
Opening wide so that he could escape.

Mercy and the Brazos River

WALT MCDONALD

My great-greats came to hardscrabble plains
when a dollar an acre was outrage. Quakers
from Iowa, they listened for God's still voice
in sandstorms, a silence under stars.
Patient, they waited for their hearts
to lead them over prairie sprawled flat
around them, a thousand miles of parchment

under the will of heaven. No trees grew native,
only buffalo grass tall enough to hold the bones
of slaughtered buffalos. If they hoped for angels
to wrestle for crops in the desert, when they found
this winding Texas stream, *Rio de los Brazos
del Dios*, they believed. Now, that canyon's

drained after decades of irrigation,
near a city of a quarter million
which pumps its gyppy water from a lake
a hundred miles away. In 1880, the dugout
where they huddled all winter was a tent
half-buried in walls of white caliche. In spite
of rattlesnakes and drought, they called it home.

The holes of prairie dogs pocked every acre.
Even the home they dug uprooted a colony of dogs.
They plugged the burrows and settled down
to stay, enough grass like pastures of heaven
for cows which survived the blizzards.
I've seen the grainy photographs, held in my hands
their beaten plows, the cracked hames of horses.

How could they leave their families for this?
What did they hope for, choking down rabbits
and snakes, enduring wind from wide horizons
without one tree, nothing but hawks in the sky
and slow whirlpools of buzzards? I've heard
the first deep well they dug was hopeless,
every dry foot like stone, and the second.

Before the third well struck an aquifer
at last, they turned enough prairie under
for a crop and a baby's grave, their plow
silver-shiny, their wagon broken often
but repaired in time to bump down that steep
caliche canyon and haul back barrels of water
from the river of the arms of God.

Inventory

LAURE-ANNE BOSSELAAR

Thanksgiving today. Soaked with sleet.
No sun for six days — six is the Devil's number.
I have looked through this window,
at these American skies for two times six years.
My wall is covered with photographs of distant friends.

This is my third garden. The first two blossomed in Belgium.
Where there is no Thanksgiving. Where my father is buried.
Where I was raised and raped and worked. Where I had five lovers,
but loved only one. Where I gave birth to three children.
A blond son, a dead daughter, a blond daughter.

Shadows grew in my first garden. Two larches in my second.
Because of North Sea winds and how they stood, they fused
into one trunk. It wounded them at first, that rubbing together —
the frailest larch losing sap for months, a lucid sap that glued them
to each other at last. I saw it as an omen for my life.

I give thanks for the lowlands in Belgium.
For Flanders, her canals and taciturn skies. For the tall ships
on the river Scheldt. For coal pyramids in Wallonia.
For the color of hop, and the hop-pickers' songs.
For Antwerp's whores who woo sailors in six different tongues.

Six is the Devil's number. My grandfather and a farmer
killed six German soldiers and threw them in a Flemish moor.
I can no longer give thanks for that: I ask mercy.
Before I die, I'll plant a larch by the moor — *miserere* —
the soldiers' mothers will never know it was done.

I prayed six times for the death of my Jew-hating father,
I ask mercy for that also: it's Thanksgiving today.
I give thanks for my son and daughter, for the man I love
who taught me a new language.
For this garden's life and sleet.

Before I left for this vast continent,
I stole sand from the river Scheldt,
an inch of barbed wire from a Concentration Camp near Antwerp,
a leaf from the chestnut tree behind Apollinaire's grave,
but no weed, not a seed of it, growing from my father's ashes.

In Belgium, the day is almost over.
Soon, a new century will make History: *miserere*.
Four larches grow in my garden: one for my son, one for my daughter —
and far from a moor in Flanders, the other two fuse
here: in America. In America.

The Pallor of Survival

LAURE-ANNE BOSSELAAR

I'm lucky: autumn is flawless today,
sidewalks freckled rust and red, and the sun
gentle. I'll take the back streets
to the bookstore — it's a longer ride — but I avoid
the street where St. John the Evangelist Church
faces that seedy building with a sign flashing
                    Jews for Jesus
The last time I pedaled between them I felt
a draft there, something so chilling I gasped.

I don't know what happened to Judith Aaron,
placed in 1945 at the Mater Immaculata convent
in Brussels, after she was repatriated from Bergen-Belzen.
Judith who waited eleven years for some — *any* —
next of kin to claim her. No one ever came
to the black and brass door. And we

never saw her again after she turned eighteen
and left that very morning, still wearing the convent
uniform, but the blouse open three buttons down
and the socks low on her white ankles. She left
on a sleety day in October, years after —
from under a bed in the infirmary — I'd seen

what the nuns did to her when she confessed
she masturbated: bending her over, pulling down
her panties to ram the longest part of an ivory crucifix
into her, hissing: HE is the Only One Who Can Come
Inside You — No One Else — You Hear?

She didn't let out a sound, not a sigh:
the pallor of survival carved into her face
when she pulled her panties up again.
I think she made it: she was of the stone
statues are made from. And yet, I still
search — Judith, I can't stop searching —
for signs we made it,
    you, me and the others,
signs I find in the smallest things:
a flawless sky, a leaf autumn
turns, an open gate.

Colors of a Free Life

MARIANNE POLOSKEY

In the war, we were always
running out of things:
sleep, food, time, hope.
All those useless summers
when the skies
sagged with planes
and colors burned away.
If the sun shone
during air raids, it seemed
God was mocking us.

Whenever someone screamed,
I thought of people
in other parts of the world
quietly raking their gardens
or sitting in outdoor cafés
over espressos with music,
reading their papers
in different languages.
People who had done
nothing wrong
and deserved a good life.
People whose dogs and cats
didn't fight.
People with plenty to eat
and dreams
rather than nightmares.
The husband went to work,
not to war. The wife
washed her hair each morning
as dew washes the grass.

Their children
were not afraid to wake up.
They trusted life, knowing
its roads would lead
wherever they expected to go.

Today, I live in the world
I used to imagine.
Still beguiled by all
the colors of a free life,
I tend the flowers
in my little garden —
velvety works of art.
Birds cheer me on
as they try out
different branches.
Like them,
I bask in the sunshine,
kissing the air with my song.

Guide to the Tokyo Subway

HALVARD JOHNSON

At Shinjuku Station
one entrance is haunted

by the spirit of a lost traveler
one who missed her train

and never found her way
around or through

that incredibly
personal disaster

passing by, I lower my head —
I who am lost every day —

feeling I ought to
have met her

*

how many foreigners
dream of walking where we do now
along the palace moat
speaking of this and that
— keep moving, keep moving —
not even wondering
where the next bottle
of beer will come from

*

there's a circle line
around the central city
on which you could ride forever
for a one-stop fare

but the trains here don't
run all night long
so you must get off somewhere
— be quiet, be quiet —
don't ask me where

⋆

in dreams
we wander through
mazes of tunnels

and passageways
underground
— hush, hush —
in the dark corridors

turnings
stairways
and escalators smoothly

sliding downward

⋆

coming up from below
my eyes take their time
adjusting to daylight

a crowd of commuters surge
past me down the steps
at a trot, at a trot

suddenly a woman stands before me
who has walked a long way
just to meet me

we have sandwiches
and tea together
before deciding to separate

leaving to others
the end of our
carefully rehearsed story

⋆

I know that at Ueno
a long time coming
cherry blossoms
glisten in lamplight
— go under, go under —
and nighttime's the best time
for viewing *sakura*, sipping *sake*

⋆

what I said
there in the station
was not what I
meant to

meanings stretch out
in all directions
turn back, turn back
on themselves

on their central
unmeaning

*

I'd always thought
that if I positioned myself
just so,
    as the train pulled
into the station
certain forces would come
into play, changing
my outlook on things
in surprising ways

the train would transport me
to a distant station
with an unfamiliar name
in an unfamiliar script
and I would get off
happy to be alive
not knowing which way to turn

Letter to Mirta Yáñez

ORLANDO RICARDO MENES

I read *Some Place in Ruins*,
your recent book of poems, and that title
seems incredibly ironic —
photograph of a Greek temple
on the cover — for our Old Habana
lies in tropical ruins; you should instead
put that colonial house
at Jesús María number 13
where my mother lived as a little girl
(abode of the ghost
Don Melitón, in life a Galician
shopkeeper)
or the Golgothas of rubble
I saw walking toward the Cathedral
on Obispo Street,
surrounded by trash and skeletal animals
(like the black dog
with the hairless tail that ate
a mango pit).
An old black woman
on Angel Hill begged me for money
to buy orange juice,
I gave her the last dollar in my pocket.

Perhaps some of her street names
could be interpreted
as omens
since Cuba crosses Anguish
and also Poor Rock.

My gray Habana,
covered with scars and wrinkles,
breath of death,
so poorly plastered and nailed together
you will soon collapse,
your only solace
ill-remembered memories.
I know you were
voluptuously beautiful,
painted with colors
of guava, papaya, and guanábana,
sassy, proud, impetuous
with carnal delights,
praised with *piropos*
(flirtatious remarks)
more vulgar than sophisticated.
The world
has scarcely noticed
your destruction,
invisible behind bars
of sugar cane.

Coral Way, Near the Roads

ORLANDO RICARDO MENES

Though this Sunday afternoon is torrid,
an old exile, fair and blue-eyed, wearing
a Chrysler cap, sits on a bus bench selling
souvenirlike paintings of La Habana Vieja.
They're rough but sensuous, his own work
perhaps. The larger canvas sits
on his lap, the miniatures lie on the bench.
Viewing them, I smile but remain silent,
and he does likewise. They portray the same scene:
a calm turquoise sea, a lone seagull flying
through a clear blue sky, and the colonial Castillo
del Morro squatting on the rocky shore.
A bright Cuban flag waves atop its parapet.

How should I respond? Should I toe the exile line
and regret the loss of a quaint, carefree Cuba?
Mi Cuba collapsed from corruption, greed, and violence.
Idyllic memories are merely a jeweled noose.

The Refugee

VIJAY SESHADRI

He feels himself at his mind's borders moving
down the fifteen rows of laid-out soil,
and out to the fence where the mulch heaps spoil
beside the rust-scabbed, dismantled swing
and the visions that disturb him sometimes spring
up from a harmless garden hose coil:
the jack-booted armies dripping spoors of oil
that slick the leaf and crap the wing . . .

He sees each rifle as we who see him,
in the crystal blizzard of a century's static,
try to reach him without two-bit magic
who escapes us to roam in the garden:
too clear to look through or distant to ask;
pinned like a flower on the genocidal past.

11. American Journeys

Homecoming

ERIC PANKEY

In time, thunder unshackles the rain.
The tassels of pollen fall. Dust,

Not breath, becomes the spirit's habit,
A finery of grit that gathers.

The jay, a blue throb in the holly,
Will scold as it bolts. What exile

Would not love the evergreen for its thorns,
The bird for the objection it sustains?

From the Book of Lamentations

ERIC PANKEY

We all have a story to tell. Mine begins
With the gift of a knife. With a road of sand.
With bees like haze above a field of thistle.

Light falls silverpoint on a parchment of straw.
Snow dusts the wings of a crow. Rude at its edges,
The season is the season-between-seasons.

I hear my father mumble through his dreams.
The hailstone placed on his tongue turns each curse to song.
No, we were never poor, my mother counters.

When she died I went through her closet and found
Five hat boxes, each stuffed with unopened bills.
My hands are stained with pollen, raw with quicklime.

There is green ice on the creek, a web's torn gauze
Across closed eyes. My sister opens the door
And a wolf enters. Hornets nest in the eaves.

A dead body, stuffed with limestone shards, still floats.
My father left my brother a heart of rain.
And the back of his hand. *Here, all this is yours:*

This cold heart of rain and the back of my hand.
Unless the stone melts or the tongue is cut clean,
A voice goes on singing its song of exile.

So long, he sang, in lamentation.
The gift of a knife is bad luck, but this blade,
Well-edged, sharp to the point, has been my fortune.

Loose Sugar

BRENDA HILLMAN

I hardly remember any sounds from childhood.
Leaving them out is second . . .

Little boys from the favelas came to the apartment for sugar.

In the smooth language I will later lose she gives it to them:

tin cupfuls to their twin existences.

   (How blind the sugar is, being passed along
and tumbling into little bodies

helplessly)

Everyone would have sacrificed something for them not
     to have to ask for it.

All our fathers stood in cane fields in some respect.

Later — the rest of my life — time resembles warm sugar,
     something almost imaginary having to do with asking.

In what part of early to hide the particular?

Those boys are dead now; in the street perhaps their children's
     children are roving bands of thieves . . .

When I was a child
in a blur   toward being better
I disagreed with the concept of "need" —

(time as short stanzas that went on
replacing each other)

Red Fingernails

BRENDA HILLMAN

Briefly I dwelt upon my mother's tongue . . .

They put up a swingset in the lobby where we liked to hang.
 Red fingernails. The polish had been an intoxicant.

Rubber trees spoke with red lips. Talking with the spirits then
 didn't seem all that necessary.

President Kubitschek is doing his best to welcome the post-
 colonial companies.

My mother rejoins her first language so she can live, and in
 making numbers, I developed a love of the partially hollow;

the other mother tried to give us her body, painting our fingernails
 in the kitchen, it was like growing sunsets.

During this time we rarely spoke English; we understood
 because of what they didn't say.

What happened is not how we should measure things.

Joy exists because there are delays:

those intervals in bodies where two languages mix

before the first one has to be lifted away —

(being truthful made the surface
sort of grainy —)

Phonograph

TODD JAMES PIERCE

And so I come to you, my uncle,
vice president of such matters,
and ask you to speak in my father's voice
because I cannot hear it any more.

I need your help
to repress the phonograph of my youth,
the long-playing silence
intermixed with conversation
and the harmonica melodies
he was able to whistle in the dark.

I need your help
to make this record I cannot find.
I've looked among yearbooks
and in boxes of clothes
that no longer fit.
Speak my name in his
scratchy, lost voice. Tell me
what you think of my wife
to be, because I would like
those words to wash over me,
a cool summer rain
puddling at my feet.

No one makes this record
anymore. I have looked
in the used stores and checked
for it on CD as well. So speak
to me, my uncle, our vice president
of such matters. Where else will I find

a bootleg, if not with you? Let your needle
of a tongue cut the groove
I so want to hear, if only
for a word, before you tell me this song
can be found on my lips as well.

My Father Learns to Speak (Again)

C. V. DAVIS

When you left the Appalachian farm for
New Haven you were afraid they would
brand you before they knew you

for months you didn't open your
mouth in class or in public
surviving by not speaking at all

the hours you spent studying theology
were far less then the hours you practiced
speech deep into early morning darkness

shortening vowels by pulling imaginary
strings on your tongue and extending
dipthongs with a short tuck of jawbone

learning how to erase your South Midland
dialect so you wouldn't sound like a slow
strum across Uncle Rickman's banjo

for the most part you succeeded

but since you've turned sixty I can hear
hills in your voice again
like when you holler at basketball games
or call from the garage for a cool drink

I wonder now why you were ashamed
what piece of yourself needed denying
what happened to your soul

but I am glad you were ordained in
New England because it meant you were
able to baptize me and marry me

and I would even let you bury me as
long as you promise to speak like you did
when you were young

a boy with a cowlick and calloused hands
safe in the valley between those mountains
you would soon leave behind

The Cloud of Unknowing

DEBORA GREGER

It is the shortest work of all that a man can imagine. It is neither
longer nor shorter than an atom which is defined . . . as the
smallest division of time, and it is so short . . . it is indivisible and
almost incomprehensible. This is the time of which it is written:
"You will be asked how you spent all the time that has been given
to you."
— The Cloud of Unknowing

Why did I not die at birth,
for then I should have lain down
    and been quiet?

I should have lain in the dirt
    beside those who fought over it,
under the ruins built in their name,

    while they lamented
the cities they destroyed and rebuilt,
    ash after ash, dust laid to dust.

I should have lain in the dirt
    looking up like the man
who put a dark cloud between himself and his god,

    the better to see him.
I should have been the woman looking up:
    the waters of the sky parting,

only a few parachutes drifting low,
    testing the wind.
And then the darkness covered the earth.

That was the second cloud.
She wiped her hands clean.
    Her skin came off in her hands.

Why did I not lie down in the river
    with the rest of them?
Invisible in the cloak of flesh,

    I should have been dust
lamenting the dust whose daughter I am.
    O dust wrapped in wind,

in the desert I found these words
    where they had burned
and put the ash on my tongue.

Exile

STEPHEN COREY

An owl calls from a brown mulberry,
Field mice fold their paws in a mess of nests.

Everywhere I turn I find homes:
Nests and burrows, sheltered corners,
Pockholes in sand, knotholes in bark.
I walk onward, only to find more homes —
Beaver cave tucked beneath its crown of dam,
Bear cave creviced on the hillside.
Beyond the path-filled, nest-filled forest,
I'll come to the closed-in city:
Sheds and shanties, mansions
In their own forests, stacks of dwellings
Rising toward the cloud-roofed sky.
I walk farther on, and farther still.
I came here to learn,
But there are days when learning means nothing.

Digging Up Peonies

VIVIAN SHIPLEY

Overcoming fear of stalks that are too close,
I remind myself it's Lexington, that mist

on fields meant rattlesnakes curled in rows
of corn would be cold, sluggish. Like prying

out potatoes with my fingers, I dig up tubers
as if I could lift my father, seeded with cancer,

if only for a day from gravity, from ground.
My parents know what I know — this is the end;

they will not return to this house my father built.
No refugee in Kosovo, wheelbarrowing

his grandmother to safety, I will bring as much
of Kentucky, of their dirt as I can carry with me

on our flight to Connecticut. A bride, moving
to New Haven over thirty years ago, I have

not taken root. I cannot explain this urge
to go to creekstone fences my father stacked,

dig up box after box of peonies I will bank
into granite piled along my side garden

so my father can see pink, fuschia blossoming
from his bed. Is this what revision is, change

of location, spreading, to retell my story
another time, in another soil? Unable to untie

what binds me to Kentucky, to bones of all
those who are in my bones, I will save what

I can of my mother, of my father from this earth,
from the dissolution that binds us after all.

Book of Ruth

CAROLYN BEARD WHITLOW

Whither thou goest . . .

I learn to live by guile, to do without love.
I'm not scared. I wait in the dark for you,
Sleeping to avoid death, tired of sleep.
　The withered dyed rug fades, dims, fades, recolors,
　Warp frayed, weft unraveled; as light looms dark,
I doubt I'm happy as can be in this house.

　Outside no one would guess inside this house
I learn to live by guise, disguise my pain. Love
Dinner served by pyre light, sit doused by dark,
　Cornered in my room, wait in the dark for you.
　The bureau melts to shadow; that unraveled, uncolors.
Sleep to avoid death, tired of sleep,

　I avoid the mirror, the lie of truth. You sleep
Downstairs, chin lobbed over, chair rocked, spilled, house
Distilled in tectonic dreams of technicolor,
　Mostly golf course green and Triumph blue. I love
　Earthpots, cattails, a fireplace, no reflection of you.
While you sleep, I sip steeped ceremonial teas, dark

　As coffee, your swirled wineglass breathing dark
Downstairs fumes in the living dead room. Sleep
Comes easy, comes easy. I'm not scared. For you
　I curtsy before your mother, say I love this house.
　I love this house, this room. I love this. I love.
The traffic light blinks black and white. No color.

　Come Monday, I'll dustmop, repaper with multicolor
Prints, zigzag zebra stripe rooms, fuchsias, no dark

Blue or sober gray, none of the colors that you love.
　　Insomnia is sweet, I think, the once I cannot sleep:
　　I'm not scared. I'm not scared. This is my house.
Illumined by darkness, I watch my dark mirror you.

　　No. No silent hostage to the dark, I know you
Cast a giant shadow in a grim fairy tale, colors
Bloodlet, blueblack, spineless yellow trim this house;
　　Escaped maroon, I emerge from a chrysalined dark,
　　Succumb, mesmerized under a light spring-fed sleep,
Nightmare over, giddy, without sleep, with love.

　　The colors of the room fade into dust, house now dark.
I'm not scared. I learn to live without you, with love,
　　To do without sleeping to avoid death, tired of sleep.

Coaching My Father on His Temporarily Moving into My Old Bedroom

MILES GARETT WATSON

When you sleep, don't pick sides —
Do it diagonal, top-right to bottom-left,
Settle into what I started years ago.
When you get up in the night, be sure you've got
Your flashlight. You can't trust your body here
To maneuver you to the bathroom.
No, don't use the cup by the sink —
It's there for show, it hasn't ever been washed.
Drink from your palm, slide water across
Your face and look yourself in the eye,
Lie and say the affair's over. Repeat it if
You have to: say it to the window in the hall,
Say it to the moonlight licking through the blinds,
Say it to my trophy case behind you, its rows of
Golden boys, each one in a perfect stance,
Bats held high and their eyes still on you,
Waiting for the next signal.

Love Penned Red

SEAN BRENDAN-BROWN

My mother finished her life in side-boxes
in shabby playhouses; she was an actress
and then she was old, and then she watched.

She had Old World grace and cut fresh flowers
each morning for Sebastian, an octogenarian who
brought ice-cold four-percent milk in bottles.

She'd laugh at this theatre — lighting wrong
music wrong, set design some novice's concept
of angst, the discomfort of a crowd

smelling each other's cured flowers, the exhaust
from the organ snuffing candles and souring breath.
Everyone thinks someone else

has ruined the tempo — she'd take responsibility,
wave off-white and marble-veined hands thumbs-up,
airbrushed blue mouth whistling

to silence that freaky, cheap-tuxedoed impresario
licking beads of sweat from his cupid's bow
and patting the coffin lid like a sideboard

he's left a deck of cards on, or his gloves.
She'd hand him a summons, *love* penned red.
That'd do it; god willing she'd be his halting place.

Lost and Found

MAXINE CHERNOFF

I am looking for the photo that would make all the difference in my life. It's very small and subject to fits of amnesia, turning up in poker hands, grocery carts, under the unturned stone. The photo shows me at the lost and found looking for an earlier photo, the one that would have made all the difference then. My past evades me like a politician. Wielding a fly-swatter, it destroys my collection of cereal boxes, my childhood lived close to the breakfast table. Only that photo can help me locate my fourteen lost children, who look just like me. When I call the Bureau of Missing Persons, they say, "Try the Bureau of Missing Photos." They have a fine collection. Here's one of Calvin Coolidge's seventh wedding. Here's one of a man going over a cliff on a dogsled. Here's my Uncle Arthur the night he bought a peacock. Oh photo! End your tour of the world in a hot air balloon. Resign your job at the mirror-testing laboratory. Come back to me, you little fool, before I find I can live without you.

Wind-Chill Factor

GLORIA VANDO
— *for Daisy Rhau*

You point to a photo of your family
taken after they fled from North Korea,
your infant mother in her father's arms,
despots pursuing them the way Uncle Sam
pursued my grandparents after confiscating
their power, their land, its yield of sugar
and coffee, iron and ore, giving them
three weeks — always three weeks! —
to relocate. Before the exodus

your mother awoke each morning
in a tepid bath, her sleeping body phased
into a basin of wrist-warm water to lessen
the shock of life, the anticipated march across
the wide divide between privilege and
anonymity — snipers, land mines at every turn.

As a child I awoke to tepid clothes,
my grandmother warming each tiny garment
with her body — my socks running a low
temperature under each arm, my panties
wedged in her cleavage, my shirt sleeves
embracing her neck, her whole body
a conduit of early morning comfort
as she dressed me under the covers,
easing me into the glare of indifference,
then rage, against an alien shade or sound.

She taught me to braid my hair, gathering
the three strands, like warring factions,
between her fingers, plaiting them over and
under and over and under until a perfect braid
emerged, my world in safe and tidy harmony.

Grown up, I wear my hair in a bun, the skill
of my grandmother's hands in mine,
weaving then coiling the long thin braid
into a perfect circle at the nape of my neck,
insulating me, still, against the chill.

Waiting on Family Court

JEFF KNORR

I know little of lawyers and courts.
The slow wait for papers processed
is like hoping for rain in summer.

So today I paint your room
and figure you'll be home soon.
I think of you in a crib a country away

and there's a drip in the door
needs brushing out. A thousand
horse hairs slide like skates

over the baseboard. I sweat
in new paint, go back and
work it in so I am in your wall,

my secret way to watch you sleep
when we're all under the thumb of night.
Later I'll slip on the ladder,

leave half a hand print high
on the wall to almost hold you on days
when I will work and you'll play.

In the corner behind the rocker
I sneeze and leave a lash in tacky
paint so I can read to you, watch,

tell you stories in summer nights
after grandfather's slick-handled
brushes are hung, away on their nails.

Jew's Harp

RODGER KAMENETZ

Held lightly against the teeth, lightly
the tongue far back must not interfere
the lips loosely cover the teeth
touch the metal with a kiss
and the breath like a sigh

To shape the notes make vowels
in the back of the throat
say them fast, run them together
and you can hear the secret name
with a breath like a sigh

The old harp and timbrels
made a joyful noise
in the temple of dust
put away long ago
The Jew's harp is cheaper now
portable instrument, easy to carry
into strange towns, across hard borders
with a breath like a sigh

Held lightly against the teeth, lightly
the word Jew muttered, not said lightly
or if at all somehow hushed, subdued,
the sound like a low whining,
hard tug or twangy gut breath,
throb, a tone deep and urgent
and a breath like a sigh

For Borscht

RODGER KAMENETZ

A bowl of borscht — sea of blood
fingers of beet — rich lump of white cream
a sour galaxy — and stars spread
their tendrils of luminous breath —

Lights in heaven and borscht in a bowl,
cold grandfather soup from the fridge
with a soft potato of maybe
spelunking in the depths,

old potato eye waiting quietly in sweet red soup.
Down comes the silver spoon to divide
the mind, down comes thought and
impotent anger, immodestly, rage and outrage —

Tears dilute the soup. Laughter shakes
the bowl, the queen of knowing and acting
who holds all in her wide and generous
embrace. More borscht please. More cold borscht.

This has to be about how one can feel
about any food, how sweet and sour mix,
and red and white. The red is from
the mother and the white is from the father,

the potato is first cousin to the beet
like grave mates side by side
in the ground. We cook the potato
in its jacket and drop it hot in the soup

but the sour cream floats down cold
and spreads its luxury slowly.
This has to be about nourishment
and desire, or about the ground and sky.

The sky in the Ukraine must have been
like this, clear blood from the heart
of beet dug from the stubborn ground.
We ate like they ate. We died

at their hands, the borscht spilling
out of our skulls, or a rivulet
from the corner of grandfather's mouth,
dribbling down his dark cotton beard.

Now imprisoned in a supermarket jar
still fresh and shining I take her home
and open her, pour sloppily, scattering
drops of her blood on the white tablecloth

borscht shekhinah, borscht mother of us all.

Yes

DENISE DUHAMEL

According to *Culture Shock:*
A Guide to Customs and Etiquette
of Filipinos, when my husband says yes,
he could also mean one of the following:
a.) *I don't know.*
b.) *If you say so.*
c.) *If it will please you.*
d.) *I hope I have said yes unenthusiastically enough*
for you to realize I mean no.
You can imagine the confusion
surrounding our movie dates, the laundry,
who will take out the garbage
and when. I remind him
I'm an American, that all his yeses sound alike to me.
I tell him here in America we have shrinks
who can help him to be less of a people-pleaser.
We have two-year-olds who love to scream "No!"
When they don't get their way. I tell him,
in America we have a popular book,
When I Say No I Feel Guilty.
"Should I get you a copy?" I ask.
He says yes, but I think he means
"If it will please you," i.e., "I won't read it."
"I'm trying," I tell him, "but you have to try too."
"Yes," he says, then makes *tampo,*
a sulking that the book *Culture Shock* describes as
"subliminal hostility . . . withdrawal of customary cheerfulness
in the presence of the one who has displeased" him.
The book says it's up to me to make things all right,
"to restore goodwill, not by talking the problem out,
but by showing concern about the wounded person's

well-being." Forget it, I think, even though I know
if I'm not nice, *tampo* can quickly escalate into *nagdadabog* —
foot stomping, grumbling, the slamming
of doors. Instead of talking to my husband, I storm off
to talk to my porcelain Kwan Yin,
the Chinese goddess of mercy
that I bought on Canal Street years before
my husband and I started dating.
"The real Kwan Yin is in Manila,"
he tells me. "She's called Nuestra Señora de Guia.
Her Asian features prove Christianity
was in the Philippines before the Spanish arrived."
My husband's telling me this
tells me he's sorry. Kwan Yin seems to wink,
congratulating me — my short prayer worked.
"Will you love me forever?" I ask,
then study his lips, wondering if I'll be able to decipher
what he means by his yes.

The Star-Spangled Banner

DENISE DUHAMEL

I was sure then, as I sang along,
that the star-spangled banner was a glittery red gown
patterned with sequin constellations
and "Oh say" was José —
a fussy lover, the kind a woman had to dress up for,
the kind who had a small well-groomed moustache
and came from a country far away from America
where romance was even more spectacular than it was here.

José, can you see
by the dancerly light
what so proudly she hails
at the twilight's last gleaming . . .

equaled this:

José is on a balcony, his tuxedo more dapper than any other.
Or maybe he is on the deck of a cruise ship. Either way,
it's sunset and his new beloved, his own Miss America,
glides towards him in her star-spangled banner . . .
His indifference to her is unbearable. *José, can you see?*
she starts to sing. A mint toothpick dangles from his lips,
his eyes gloss over and he's in a place countries away
where all the other Josés are roasting meat over an open flame,
where señoritas huddle together in their fan-and-castanet glamour.

Who brought mites and bright stars
to the perilous fight?
All the remnants she bought
were so gallantly gleaming . . .

The red-dressed woman is used to having men notice her.
She starts to complain, whine really, interrupting José's
nostalgic dreaming. He can't stand her voice
so he clobbers his boring demanding American girlfriend
and she blinks cartoon stars, tiny flies
circling her head like planes waiting to land.
He doesn't know why he hits her exactly
except that maybe her kisses don't taste spicy enough.
He says, "You're American, I thought you were rich!"
as she fusses over a star that's fallen off her dress
and explains she made her flamenco gown herself
with material she bought on sale at a fabric store
that was going out of business in her small American town.
José's guilty hands cover his face.
He tells her he's never hit a woman before
as she pops up from the ground like a buxom Roadrunner
and shakes her coiffed head from side to side.
José reaches out his hand to help her as she lifts
her star-spangled skirt. Her legs whirl faster than fan blades
and she is off, zooming across America, leaving José
choking in the cloud of dust she trails.

José, does that star-spangled banner yet wave?

Do you miss her, José?
Do you miss the dress she sewed thinking of you?
Did you stick around the United States
or return to a place where the women know
exactly how to please their Josés,
where your waxy facial hair will forever be in style?

She told me to tell you, José, that she forgives everything
and hopes that you're happy.
She hopes, too, that you can forgive her first-grade self
for creating you out of a song where you didn't even exist

and then having you do some pretty crummy things.
Please know that your would-be American girlfriend
still pines for you, José, somewhere in Nebraska or North Dakota.
She has a slew of kids now and her red dress is in storage.
She cries when she watches reruns of I Love Lucy,
Ricky's accent so much like how she remembers yours.

Translating My Parents

ALLISON JOSEPH

When my father would growl,
wash the wares now, I always thought
he'd said w-e-d-s, learned to move
to the sink quickly, in terror,

knew his order meant
wash the dishes right away,
and don't use too much soap.
And when Mother asked me

to put serviettes on the table,
I knew she meant set the table,
use napkins, the paper kind.
What sort of English was this

that they spoke so surely,
an odd lingo of strange terms
like brolly and dustbin
for umbrella and trashcan,

flannel instead of washcloth,
plimsolls instead of sneakers?
Baffled by their love
of fish and chips, crisps

and crumpets, I wondered
why they drank tea instead of coffee,
why my father downed Guinness
instead of Miller High Life,

making me sip that dark bitter stout,
laughing as I grimaced, wrinkling
my eight-year-old nose. I couldn't
imagine them living in any other

country but this one, in any other
house but this one, couldn't imagine
the house of my birth — 289 Wightman Road,
London borough of Haringey.

The only borough I knew was the Bronx,
and there an elevator was an elevator,
not a lift, a cookie was a cookie,
not a biscuit, and no one dared call

sausage and potatoes "bangers and mash."
I learned to translate their dialect
into an English I could recognize,
so when my father nagged

write a zed, and write it properly,
I knew he truly meant write a Z,
as in zipper, as in zero, and write
it plainly, so I can read it.

Arturo

MARIA MAZZIOTTI GILLAN

I told everyone
your name was Arthur,
tried to turn you
into the imaginary father
in the three-piece suit
that I wanted instead of my own.
I changed my name to Marie,
hoping no one would notice
my face with its dark Italian eyes.

Arturo, I send you this message
from my younger self, that fool
who needed to deny
the words
(Wop! Guinea! Greaseball!)
slung like curved spears,
the anguish of sandwiches
made from spinach and oil;
the roasted peppers on homemade bread,
the rice pies of Easter.

Today, I watch you,
clean as a cherub,
your ruddy face shining,
closed by your growing deafness
in a world where my words
cannot touch you.

At 80, you still worship
Roosevelt and JFK,
read the newspaper carefully,

know with a quick shrewdness
the details of revolutions and dictators,
the cause and effect of all wars,
no matter how small.
Only your legs betray you
as you limp from pillar to pillar,

yet your convictions remain
as strong now as they were at 20.
For the children, you carry chocolates
wrapped in goldfoil
and find for them always
your crooked grin and a $5 bill.

I smile when I think of you.
Listen, America,
this is my father, Arturo,
and I am his daughter, Maria.
Do not call me Marie.

Lenox Hill

AGHA SHAHID ALI

In Lenox Hill Hospital, after surgery, my
mother said the sirens sounded like the
elephants of Mihiragula when his men drove
them off cliffs in the Pir Panjal Range.

The Hun so loved the cry, one falling elephant's,
he wished to hear it again. At dawn, my mother
heard, in her hospital-dream of elephants,
sirens wail through Manhattan like elephants
forced off Pir Panjal's rock cliffs in Kashmir:
the soldiers, so ruled, had rushed the elephants.
The greatest of all footprints is the elephant's,
said the Buddha. But not lifted from the universe,
those prints vanished forever into the universe,
though nomads still break news of those elephants
as if it were just yesterday the air spread the dye
("War's annals will fade into night / Ere their story die"),

the punishing khaki whereby the world sees us die
out, mourning you, O massacred elephants!
Months later, in Amherst, she dreamt: she was, with dia-
monds, being stoned to death. I prayed: If she must die,
let it only be some dream. But there were times, Mother,
while you slept, that I prayed, "Saints, let her die."
Not, I swear by you, that I wished you to die
but to save you as you were, young, in song in Kashmir,
and I, one festival, crowned Krishna by you, Kashmir
listening to my flute. You never let gods die.
Thus I swear, here and now, not to forgive the universe
that would let me get used to a universe

without you. She, she alone, was the universe
as she earned, like a galaxy, her right not to die,

defying the Merciful of the Universe,
Master of Disease, "in the circle of her traverse"
of drug-bound time. And where was the god of elephants,
plump with Fate, when tusk to tusk, the universe,
dyed green, became ivory? Then let the universe,
like Paradise, be considered a tomb. Mother,
they asked me, *So how's the writing?* I answered *My mother
is my poem.* What did they expect? For no verse
sufficed except that promise, fading, of Kashmir
and the cries that reached you from the cliffs of Kashmir

(across fifteen centuries) in the hospital. *Kashmir,
she's dying!* How her breathing drowns out the universe
as she sleeps in Amherst. Windows open on Kashmir:
There, the fragile wood-shrines — so far away — of Kashmir!
O Destroyer, let her return there, if just to die.
Save the right she gave its earth to cover her, Kashmir
has no rights. When the windows close on Kashmir,
I see the blizzard-fall of ghost-elephants.
I hold back — she couldn't bear it — one elephant's
story: his return (in a country far from Kashmir)
to the jungle where each year, on the day his mother
died, he touches with his trunk the bones of his mother.

"As you sit here by me, you're just like my mother,"
she tells me. I imagine her: a bride in Kashmir,
she's watching, at the Regal, her first film with Father.
If only I could gather you in my arms, Mother,
I'd save you — now my daughter — from God. The universe
opens its ledger. I write: How helpless was God's mother!
Each page is turned to enter grief's accounts. Mother,
I see a hand. *Tell me it's not God's. Let it die.*
I see it. It's filling with diamonds. Please let it die.
Are you somewhere alive, weeping for me, Mother?
Do you hear what I once held back: in one elephant's
cry, by his mother's bones, the cries of those elephants

that stunned the abyss? Ivory blots out the elephants.
I enter this: *The Belovéd leaves one behind to die.*
For compared to my grief for you, what are those of Kashmir,
and what are (I close the ledger) the griefs of the universe
when I remember you — beyond all accounting — O my mother?

My Father Recounts a Story from His Youth

KEVIN PRUFER

He who discovered
three tektites along the sheer banks
of Crater Lake, mounted them
above the fish tank,
who unearthed four hundred flint
ceremonial blades from the muck
of a neolithic lake,
in central Ohio, photographed them,
put them in a book,
this is the story as he told it
to me:
         He was just eighteen, younger
than I am now, beardless,
his father vanished
to Switzerland, his mother
dying in Baden Baden.
The Brazilian summer had stained him
brown as the village boys who played
on the ancient cistern wall below.
At his feet were pottery shards
painted in green whorls.
The day he spent in the quiet
sun, piecing them together
for the older archaeologists.
The water was clear and deep —
the village boys raced
along its edge, raced and fell.
From the hill above, my father
could hear them laughing,
shouting their foreign
exclamations.

It was their cries
rising, faint, distorted
on the wind, that caught his attention.
Those shimmering figures,
six of them, each alike,
black-haired, child-like —
and the first leaped into the still water.
My father counted the seconds, but the boy
did not resurface. The second jumped
laughing, and did not reappear. So it went
with the other four, each leaping
from the stone wall, vanishing
into the green water.
                    In my family
we are all susceptible.
My sister often wakes
to see our dead grandmother
standing over her bed with a cup
of tea, smiling in the dark.
My cousin imagined his room
filling with water. He climbed
onto the window ledge fifteen storeys high
to save himself. Even I
have seen figures disappearing
into the curtains, or the red-faced
old man crying on the street corner,
nowhere in sight when
I look again.
                    My father
draws this conclusion:
You could vanish like that, he says,
into the green waters of wherever
you go. He holds onto me then,
or he takes me to his study
in the back of the house. This,

he says, holding a round black stone,
is a tektite, four billion years old.
This is a projectile point, white quartz,
quite rare.
      Sometimes he tells me
about the six Brazilian boys.
We're all going that way, he says.
Outside, it is raining, drops splattering
on the skylights. There is nothing
permanent in this world, he says —
and he is surrounded by everything that is.

Jasmine

GEORGE KALAMARAS

There is no beginning and no end
to it, at least to the jasmine blossoms
she leans into in the court and shows
you. You want her to teach you
that highly developed sense of female
smell, how she can detect a gas leak
even amidst curry at home, or know
the dog's been rolling in dead birds, or sense
the coming of roses, but you don't know how
to ask. You shuffle out of your hotel
instead, hail a rickshaw and turn
to her, *Yeah, nice jasmines,* knowing you missed
some scent that might make you
whole and could save the world
if sniffed just right. Your entire life
you've struggled with it, how to say *no*
when you mean *no*, how to read the news
and stop the flood, how to stare at the phone
with perfect calm and not answer
and not run from room to room. You're six again
and crying when it rings, only this time inside
where the acid from your coffee stirs
My Friend Flicka and she kicks up
dust and the '62 Chevy is always
brand new. That eternal hope
of Lassie, say, or Rin Tin Tin and new-car
smell in the way they lick a hand
and with a whimper make the healing
begin. You step onto the silver lip
of the rickshaw, feeling your weight,
sensing the odor of decades of sweat

on the cart seat, in the torn burlap
canopy that tousles your hair and makes you
feel like a kid at a wedding, smells
of possibility and pain in the musky cake
cutting and wine and slow-touching hips
of the last song, in the perfume
that lingers on the garter
and scent of silk that high, odors you don't yet know
the language of, like Hindi scrawled
in rain-soaked leather of the wallah's bicycle
seat, but older, say, like Sanskrit
script and lost. Where can you look,
you wonder, to decode the directions
for smell, even if it is red vinyl, ripped
and sun-bleached like old blood? Even
if it is the oil of so many unknown heads
rubbing up against yours through the sag
of the canopy, like dogs trying to find their way
among one another on the street? So you step onto
the lip and crush the seat and examine the sweat
that drips from the rickshaw wallah's lungi
wrapped around thighs, tucked between legs,
from the cracked rubber and salt-spill
of his thongs, from the peddling up hill
that always makes your shoulders ache afterwards
at night when you look in the mirror.
You want to smell it all, to know when
the bird has fallen, to anticipate
the roses, to bury the stallions
and pick up the receiver
for once without the dust and kicking
in your gut. To turn toward your wife
and graze her palm where the scent
remains in cracks like star charts
we are given to learn

the birth of blossoms
and thorns, the new and the torn.
To smell jasmine in an uphill
climb and enormous dignity
in the difficult smile
given — even sweetness in the reaching for a rupee
and in the sudden turning and peddling away,
in burnt curry and crust in bottoms
of street-corner cauldrons or the wok
back home, and in the gas leak
that occasionally comes to remind you
who and what you are.

Dislocation

RALPH ADAMO

We move the word into the river
vary the wood the box is composed of
strong air in still life

Don't we want that goddamned word
to float, and to float senselessly to sea

★★★★★ ★★★★★ ★★★★★

All the words for grief and love
deposed, disposed of, indisposed

Moving the river through the small word
"river," she beholds her house

★★★★★ ★★★★★ ★★★★★

She changes her mind

Death is not necessary, nor is suffering
an art, nor continuity the virtue
it once seemed.
       Seamed through the veins
of her lover lying there his words arrest
so madly on her own that both lie
very still, very little breathing between
their acts of sacrifice, filaments
for the drawn out tune remorse and she
leaves him their sweetly lethal devices
tuned, all turned, all not, not all

the broken words for what flowed,
what flew the blue shallows, what fucking
was there, fierce and unshrewed —
center of the both of her swaying song-
like and likened, blood without the usual
measure. We take our kisses for the night
itself, our giving over for the day the night
intersects. Who could imagine
the end of love at the beginning, who
would still keep the wax within his eyes
from melting, the word itself from speaking?

***** ***** *****

No matter. What was happy was not
happy, what was balm only burns, only
ever burned. The light goes out upon
the word "river," descends to ground below
the liquid she once swam through meeting him.
Those words mean nothing now, no
words, all words, mean nothing, nothing
now, now parted, like the river aslant
a skyfull of wood burned down.

She calls herself home. Exactly what
he calls her, calls her, calling to her,
calling into the black space where she
had traveled, the time and space she'd
come now, all broken, a mad littering.

He cannot have her or his own sorrow.
He cannot have any of it. She
has it all dropped into the river
below the river, below the calm house
that is hers and hers alone or not

alone, but hers in a waterfall the words
cannot penetrate, their bright opacity
her familiar, the flow her flow, the word —
if there ever were a word — deeply silenced.

How to Look West from Mount Pleasant, Utah

SETH TUCKER

Your brushstrokes licked dryly at cheap canvas
in raspy, natural swipes; on brown and green Army
shirts stretched between boards — some obscure affront
to the precipitous mountains of the Wasatch Front. The weeping
of your brush was nearly audible, one treacherous
vision of the world after another. Your first painting
was cartoonishly symmetrical. A row of hills like
the inverted udders of the sows you raised. This one is lost.
What is left is unfinished. A legacy of unharvested fruit,
an Indian Summer snowstorm, a B-2 flying in low, bringing with it
a modern nuclear dogma. A field lingers, white with alkaline salt,
where the bones of a dinosaur wait, feet up and eyes rolling
in the back of their sockets.

What remains is a farmhouse, or church, rising from a bitter hillside;
it is buried in sharp snowdrifts. There are buried plows and shredders
and combines under there. Their metallic ears point to the empty sky
like cactus. You are there, on the steps looking off, away
from the mountains west, at what remains of the frontier;
or maybe, at the last frozen crow, climbing up from the dead
barley and hay. There are no sounds there. No radio ever
whispered to the three sets of children growing all wildly different.
Who was there to remind you of the year? Was it 1943 or 1945?
These numbers must have seemed alien — a gift from the future.
Maybe you are not looking, but listening, to the sound of
one million four-hundred thousand lost voices.

The questions remain the same. How will this be written
to sound important, like the gray caribou is important,
or the trap-door spider? Important like cheese, in soft
curds, stirring in stainless steel, tripping and burping

their way among milk solids. Why purple? Why make the sky
the color of granite, and the mountains the color of
my eye when that neighbor kid punched it. The yellow too,
of a bruise, on the cloudbank. It could have been anyone's
bruise color, but it felt like mine. How could you keep
your back turned to that color, and the reaching, the way
the mountains reach for your shoulder, to touch you, saying
hey animal, that is my abdomen you stand on, or *This bald patch*
(you know, the one to the west of the Snake River) *itches*
like a mother-fucker.

Even on the porch, your hands are curled to the reins
of a horse, or to the huge ladle in the cheese factory,
or around the neck of a chicken. The house behind
you seems empty. Painted empty in moribund fascination,
painted empty among squadrons of children, empty
and hollow like a casket, and yes, there is a better metaphor
but I have seen that house you grew up in and it seemed
drafty and wet and empty, like a casket, the wooden kind
that lets one's remains leak out after only one week. That
is why you stand out in the cold (November?) looking west,
away from the mountains, toward what remains of
the frontier, away from the house you were raised in, and
where you raised children, and where on some evenings
your wife would wash your aching feet — peeling off
the moldy boots, whispering *Poor, poor Daddy* from
the milking stool.

You stayed home, the only male left to listen to a silence
so profound it maddened the hounds, and the moose,
and pulled trees down in squealing ecstasy. The white
of the snow seems dirty around the porch steps, as if
the world was set upon something else. A river ran nearby, the
sound of it melting was morose and languid. Are you listening
to it complain about the Frenchmen who hunt its waters

for the beaver and the otter? Your expression is one I have seen
before — it is the blank expression that pursed your lips and wrinkled
your brow wherever you tried to solve the triangle peg puzzle that
Grandma gave you. You laughed when I told you a peg was missing,
when I said it was impossible. You said, "That remains to
be seen."

Now, when I look at this painting, I wonder what would
have happened if,
instead of looking west,
you had been looking down —
at what the color of soil
                    looks like on canvas.

Heat Wave: Liberty, Missouri

CAROLYNE WRIGHT

I can't wait to see
that evening sun go down.
In this first-floor hotbox,
no Billie or Bessie or Big Mama Thornton
to remind me where we've been:

New Orleans, easy city
where a white woman's dark-skinned lover
could disappear into the Creole wards
while the nay-sayers shrugged
and went on pruning the brown leaves
from their family trees. City

where we walked home from the Quarters
past the multicolored stalls
of the fruit and flower market,
cries of the Cajun vendors.
Where we shot the bolt of our blue-
shuttered flat in the Faubourg-Marigny
and made love under the ceiling fan
as midsummer rainstorms swept the yards
and lightning touched down around us.

Here, derailed from my big-city expectations,
I'm on my own.
Whatever I choose to make of it.
Every suitcase I unpack
a concession.

Dogs in the front yards
bark at my accent and my bedroom-

colored skin, the red dress
I wear Thursdays that says
I don't give a damn. Through jalousies
the neighborhood watches — I'm part
of all that's wrong with America.

Only the radio gives the facts.
Twenty years to the day
from Selma. Twenty years from the hoses,
dogs, the demonstrators lying in rows
in the squad cars' shadows.
Two blocks from the Kappa Alpha house
with the Confederate flag
hanging between white columns.

Every night, someone stands under my window
smoking Camels. I lower the bedframe
from its closet, sleep in a room
with screens unlocked
and a fan that drowns out
the footfalls of intruders.
Every morning, I get right up
against day's burning wall,
the *I Have a Dream* speech
fading from air above the marchers.

What else could we have said
even if I believed my life here?
If I dreamed the crossed sticks
on the lawn, waiting for evening
to burst into spontaneous flame?
One signature in the wrong place
and this old world of have-to's
got me good, twenty years
from the Freedom Riders
and Rosa Parks's *I'm tired.*

We know which side this town took.
My parents are proud
of how far from you I've come,
justifying the looped shadow
that falls down between us.
They don't see how I stand
before the bedroom mirror,
touching my nipples to the glass.

You, If No One Else

TINO VILLANUEVA

— *Tú, por si no otro, translated by James Hoggard*

Listen, you
who transformed your anguish
into healthy awareness,
put your voice
where your memory is.
You who swallowed
the afternoon dust,
defend everything you understand
with words.
You, if no one else,
will condemn with your tongue
the erosion each disappointment brings.

You, who saw the images
of disgust growing,
will understand how time
devours the destitute;
you, who gave yourself
your own commandments,
know better than anyone
why you turned your back
on your town's toughest limits.

Don't hush,
don't throw away
the most persistent truth,
as our hard-headed brethren
sometimes do.
Remember well
what your life was like: cloudiness,
and slick mud

after a drizzle;
flimsy windows the wind
kept rattling
in winter, and that
unheated slab dwelling
where coldness crawled
up in your clothes.

Tell how you were able to come
to this point, to unbar
History's doors
to see your early years,
your people, the others.
Name the way
rebellion's calm spirit has served you,
and how you came
to unlearn the lessons
of that teacher,
your land's omnipotent defiler.

Remember how,
from the first emptiness,
you started saving yourself,
and ask yourself what,

after all,

these words are good for
in this round hour now
where your voice strikes time.

A Note on My Son's Face

TOI DERRICOTTE

I.

Tonight, I look, thunderstruck
at the gold head of my grandchild.
Almost asleep, he buries his feet
between my thighs;
his little straw eyes
close in the near dark.
I smell the warmth of his raw
slightly foul breath, the new death
waiting to rot inside him.
Our breaths equalize our heartbeats;
every muscle of the chest uncoils,
the arm bones loosen in the nest
of nerves. I think of the peace
of walking through the house,
pointing to the name of this, the name of that,
an educator of a new man.

Mother. Grandmother. Wise
Snake-woman who will show the way;
Spider-woman whose black tentacles
hold him precious. Or will tear off his head,
her teeth over the little husband,
the small fist clotted in trust at her breast.

This morning, looking at the face of his father,
I remembered how, an infant, his face was too dark,
nose too broad, mouth too wide.
I did not look in that mirror
and see the face that could save me
from my own darkness.

Did he, looking in my eye, see
what I turned from:
my own dark grandmother
bending over gladioli in the field,
her shaking black hand defenseless
at the shining cock of flower?

I wanted that face to die,
to be reborn in the face of a white child.

I wanted the soul to stay the same,
for I loved to death,
to damnation and God-death,
the soul that broke out of me.
I crowed: My Son! My Beautiful!
But when I peeked in the basket,
I saw the face of a black man.

Did I bend over his nose
and straighten it with my fingers
like a vine growing the wrong way?
Did he feel my hand in malice?
Generations we prayed and fucked
for this light child,
the shining god of the second coming;
we bow down in shame
and carry the children of the past
in our wallets, begging forgiveness.

11.
A picture in a book,
a lynching.
The bland faces of men who watch
a Christ go up in flames, smiling,
as if he were a hooked

fish, a felled antelope, some
wild thing tied to boards and burned.
His charring body
gives off light — a halo
burns out of him.
His face is scorched featureless;
the hair matted to the scalp
like feathers.
One man stands with his hand on his hip,
another with his arm
slung over the shoulder of a friend,
as if this moment were large enough
to hold affection.

III.
How can we wake
from a dream
we are born into,
that shines around us,
the terrible bright air?

Having awakened,
having seen our own bloody hands,
how can we ask forgiveness,
bring before our children the real
monster of their nightmares?

The worst is true.
Everything you did not want to know.

Photo, 1945

FRANCISCO ARAGÓN

The only photo of you black and white
and torn — the frayed edge
climbing your chest, just missing

your left eye, cutting
off your ear: only your face
was spared. The link

is your daughter, youngest
of eleven. Lifting
the hem of her cotton dress

above her knees, she lowers herself
onto the pebbles and beans
you've carefully arranged

on the ground. Sitting nearby
you raise your head, peering
over the pages of La Prensa

to discipline a child with your eyes:
until you think she's had enough,
she kneels perfectly still . . .

Later, you rise from your chair
and stretch, noting in the distance
a slice of sun, how it hovers

over Momotombo, smearing fire
across a jagged horizon:
time for drinks and a game

of cards, when a certain mood
seeps into your skin. Hurry, they're waiting
for you to deal the first hand.

Summer air laced with the sounds
of insects soon fills
with the small bells of Pedro's

approaching cart, peddling the ice
he scrapes and then flavors
with syrup. Knowing you well, she

scrambles to the table,
your chair, but you're ahead of her:
having heard the jingling too,

you've set aside a few *córdobas*
next to your tin cup of beer.
Your large dark hand cups

the back of my mother's head
as you kiss her forehead
in front of your friends, pressing

the coins into her palm . . . Abuelo,
I'm holding you
in my fingers — the broken window

you gaze from, a face
I've never really seen,
or touched.

Auger

R. T. SMITH

Through cold salt wash
and the bilge stench
of steerage, across a fast

as stern as starving,
my great-grandfather
pursuing a bright future

dragged his canvas satchel
of carpenter's tools,
but only the Irish oak

handle and its black iron
spiral remain, the heft
oiled with his sweat,

and in the dream that comes
with storms, I lift
the auger in my hands

to drill through the lid
of a coffin he wrought
at sea. At last, I can gaze

just once upon the face
of his young Galway wife
and wonder what else

was lost with adze and saw,
the silk soprano of her voice,
a beechwood rosary

and — as if to say the cost
is always more than any
waking heart can lock in place —

the crewel shawl
she was making in the dark
of her hard berth. He saved

and passed to me — as if
to praise her craft and say,
promise to honor our ghosts —

one scrap of limerick lace.
In the throes of dream at least
I listen and obey.

Ghost Passenger, Day and Night

MICHAEL DENNISON

Each morning, I wake batlike upside down,
see everything starkly in black and white,
decipher every pocket nook hole cranny
in the train coach. Every seal is broken,
every secret is plain every secret indifferent
to me.

Outside, the larks swoop in the arc of locomotives
and nightingales sing in the black knobs of coal
below Polish Hill. Not even the crack of morning
breaks their sweet, persistent song.

The tint, but not the sheen, is blanched
from the red silk curtains on the coach windows.
I want you to see it like I do.

(It cannot be long before you join me,
already all the things you love are deadly,
you can only talk slowly; I hear you wrestling
for control and yet more control.)

Me, I was not ready or quick when my angel,
a platinum blonde with silver eyes and black lips,
raised these silk blinds to point out darkest stars.
I said then I wanted to be cold, invisible,
padding everywhere in bedroom slippers,
from train to new platform to train
with my old, gray Samsonite holding a change of clothes,
photographs from old love affairs, and maps
to all the tracks and cities of the Americas.

At night in the dark coach cars, I read your newspapers,
one from a different city every night:
New York Pittsburgh Cleveland Chicago Omaha,
all cities where I loved best as I knew how.

Mornings in the club car I wonder that each day seems new
rattling over the same tracks beside county highways.
With a rush of conscience, I watch you drive to your office
and I know above us something with omniscience watches us
with the diamonded vision of a spider
noting the descent of fat, blue flies.

And somehow I find a corresponding memory of touch
with this suggestion of your eyes at the window.
And later, before detraining, I write
in smoke on every mirror where I hope
you will see it:
the face in here is here to stay,
even after the light is gone.

Thoreau

TIMOTHY LIU

My father and I have no place to go.
His wife will not let us in the house —
afraid of catching AIDS. She thinks
sleeping with men is more than a sin,
my father says, as we sit on the curb
in front of someone else's house.
Sixty-four years have made my father
impotent. Silver roots, faded black
dye mottling his hair make him look
almost comical, as if his shame
belonged to me. Last night we read
Thoreau in a steak house down the road
and wept: "If a man does not keep pace
with his companions, let him travel
to the music that he hears, however
measured or far away." The orchards
are gone, his village near Shanghai
bombed by the Japanese, the groves
I have known in Almaden — apricot,
walnut, peach, and plum — hacked down.

The Minks

TOI DERRICOTTE

In the backyard of our house on Norwood,
there were five hundred steel cages lined up,
each with a wooden box
roofed with tar paper;
inside, two stories, with straw
for a bed. Sometimes the minks would pace
back and forth wildly, looking for a way out;
or else they'd hide in their wooden houses, even when
we'd put the offering of raw horse meat on their trays, as if
they knew they were beautiful
and wanted to deprive us.
In spring the placid kits
drank with glazed eyes.
Sometimes the mothers would go mad
and snap their necks.
My uncle would lift the roof like a god
who might lift our roof, look down on us
and take us out to safety.
Sometimes one would escape.
He would go down on his hands and knees,
aiming a flashlight like
a bullet of light, hoping to catch
the orange gold of its eyes.
He wore huge boots, gloves
so thick their little teeth couldn't bite through.
"They're wild," he'd say. "Never trust them."
Each afternoon when I put the scoop of raw meat rich
with eggs and vitamins on their trays,
I'd call to each a greeting.
Their small thin faces would follow as if slightly curious.
In fall they went out in a van, returning

sorted, matched, their skins hanging down on huge metal
hangers, pinned by their mouths.
My uncle would take them out when company came
and drape them over his arm—the sweetest cargo.
He'd blow down the pelts softly
and the hairs would part for his breath
and show the shining underlife which, like
the shining of the soul, gives us each
character and beauty.

Postcards from Florida

LARRY WAYNE JOHNS

The vertical blinds separate and come back together
like gills, as cool air spills from the ceiling vents.
Scattered among pines and palms
are these strange notched and crabbed trees
I've never seen before. Mother,
the Spanish moss shifting in the wind
looks like shredded nests.
I've barely begun to unpack.

*

I'm sorry he won't speak to you.
On the phone Dad and I talked about the weather, as usual.
He asked about the forest fires
then told me he wants to be cremated,
his ashes scattered in the backyard.
He spoke about wiping Nana's forehead
with a damp cloth, slipping a piece of ice
around the web of tubes
into her parched mouth. He said *She mouthed
morphine and shook her head no.*
I listened until his voice broke.

*

My face is burnt from a trip to St. George Island.
On the way we passed New Life Pentecostal
and Mount Trial Primitive Baptist.
The handpainted signs were faded and peeling
in the towns we drove through: *Carrabelle,*
meaning beautiful square, and *Panacea,*
a remedy for all diseases.

*

Crossing the long bridge to the island
there's a sign: *Drive slow,*
endangered shore birds nesting.
I saw them on the sides: black crests
and orange beaks, a flock of royal terns.
Of course, some cars refused to slow down,
and remains were being pecked
by fish crows. Pelicans perched
on what was left of a sunken pier.

⋆

I'll be praying that Dad's blood work comes back
with good news. How's he doing?
How are you, Mother? All's well here.
But the Apalachicola forest is still burning.
I can smell the smoke.
On the front page of the newspaper, a picture
of women at the First Church of God, arms raised,
palms upturned. The caption said, "PRAYERS FOR RAIN."
I read firefighters contained the blaze,
forcing a section to burn itself out.
They said wild fires can be good for the forest
by clearing the understory,
allowing more light to reach the ground.

Vanity of the Atlantic Ocean

JOHN BRADLEY

— *for my grandfather, Michael Xidas*

Face it, Michael. She never loved you. The ocean with as many lovers as there are men who rolled in her arms. In New York City, you, a boy of only twelve, recognized her, the scent of the woman reaching for ginger-root, that smell of sweat, salt water, the far away. Face it, she never loved you, she only wanted to take away what you never had.

Kriti, or was it Khios? Your postage stamp of an island, thimbleful of Greece. They might as well have buried you at your funeral deep in some shaft dug into the Atlantic, and lowered you down past the rows of windows, where your relatives watched and wept. Then, at last, hearing yourself speak as the water rushed past your lips, you might have remembered some of what was forgot.

A woman scratches her name into a ledger, and thus, with the hand of the undertaker, writes the place of her birth on her death certificate. Grandfather, you who my eyes touched but cannot remember, what is there for me to forget? That ocean, bursting your brain, washing away the name of your village, your childhood sweetheart, everything that made you more than a glassful of ocean, a shiver of seaweed. She did this to you, grandfather. She, with nothing to remember, nothing to forget.

And so, you crossed her, chewing willow bark to numb your insides. And what of Greece did you bring with you? Twelve years, poured, cup by cup, through the soles of your feet, until your nose began to bleed. That Greece passed down to me from between the legs of my mother when I, part-Greek, was born.

Atlantic Ocean, part-animal, part-vegetable, part-mineral, part-unspeakable light. Translucent skin that separates red from white wine, red blood cells from white. Behind every grandfather, every immigrant, one ocean, the same one that divides Greece from America, grandfather and grandson, heartbeat from heart.

You took away his Greece and left him — what? America, a grocery store in Charleston, a wife who refused to speak. You took away Michael Peter Xidas and left no memory of the boy who rose one morning and crossed the Atlantic in his red leather shoes that curl up at the toes, the way memory spills when you try to remember, and all you get is sexless salt, bisected water.

For the Old Rider at the Mall in Sioux Falls

DONALD MORRILL

I didn't have change for a jug of Thunderbird
when, drunk and busted by your old bulls,
you yelled *Quicksand!*
I made you, sonofabitch,
kowtow! and had me by the arm, mumbled rodeo,
and hugged my neck as I tried to back away.
I kept smiling at passers-by,
but I must have looked like your boy,
come for the old man and used to the sour breath
of a life story trying to escape.
You clutched my collar like a strap
as I yanked out from under your dead weight.
And your grip minus two fingers was strong enough
to almost strip half of me
as you fell, face banging the tile,
and I dragged off toward the parking lot and home.
I knew then the world is full of drunks and people holding on,
and people stopping sometimes to imagine why.
But I ditched that ripped shirt in my neighbor's trash can,
my anger useless as a consolation prize.
Some gate opens when I feel those few seconds rustle,
barely harnessed by recall or fortune.
Then Quicksand, fevered, bucks riderless into flight,
and in the dirt those two pinched-off fingers lie
like a warning to let go or be thrown.
Whoever you are you may still be dying,
somewhere sprawling to the dust.
I can only guess, no longer anyone's boy
but in moments like this,
when suddenly you appear
and I am already wrenching away

half exposed to the future —
where every beast I dream
breaking you
is ours,
and the helpless thing lives, bruising, human.

Mexican

RAY GONZALEZ

There was an eagle high above the painted sorrow.

How do you know what this means?

I spell like the monkey of anger.

Can you follow the flute as it crashes into the well of ruins?

There was a trail cut into the red mountain
where my father stayed.
He dwelled there without anger or disease.
He took women in, ate out
of clean bowls and cut his hair with a torch,
made me obey him, showed me
how to cut my own hair.
He never spoke about his lies or myths,
lived as if the world understood him.
He walked out one day.
I did not follow.

How can you forgive the belly button?

I ate the flesh from the bone.
I traced his outline in the dirt and stood back.

Can you follow him and still be his son?

There was an eagle high above the painted chair.

How many sons have sat there?

I saw a fire in the desert and watched it spread.
No one put it out and it covered the world.
The smoke entered our house and removed my sins.
There was an eagle in the black cloud of smoke.
I thought I saw it, but I could have been wrong.
I have been teaching my son who was never born.

A man killed a snake with his bare feet.

How did he know the fang belonged to him?

There was a man cutting the bite on his leg with a knife.
He spit the poison at my feet.
I held onto his shoulders and sweating head.
I thought I knew who he was, but he disappeared.
He told me about the oncoming jungle
and took the first train.

Did he know where the tracks were going?

He knew how to jump from the moving train.

When did he get off?

He was found in the boxcar full of
suffocated men and women.
He was the only one alive.

Did he get rid of the snake poison?

I can't answer what has not touched me
because I grew up without a father.
He entered walls in silence and dwelled there.
His black hair turned white, then back to black.
His body was fat, then thin.

He belted me hard so I could see,
made me money, food, the power
to silence his sins in me.

I grew older thinking the eagle fell between father and son.
I had no choice, but died without a father.
He was a burial mound, the deep grave of the eagle,
a place neither my father nor I have seen,
because we are not sons of snakebitten men
digging themselves out of the ground.

How do you know this is true?

I can retell this without staring at the floor.
If I look up on the wall, I will see the largest,
whitest moth I have ever seen.

To the Bougainvillaea

C. DALE YOUNG

How could I have imagined your absence?
In England, you do not haunt the streets.
Only weeds bloom in the cracks of sidewalks

to throw their white spindles on my shoes.
And what day could be complete without you,
your random reds, the way you climbed fences,

you, the rambunctious one,
the permanent guest of the stationary,
half-sister to the vines,

clinging where you were least expected?
In the window, my hair is white.
The islands did not prepare me:

how little I understood *white* there,
the waves of it breaking against the shoreline,
and everywhere bougainvillaea, bougainvillaea.

The Patriot

CHRISTOPHER DAVIS

Confused, using no maps, oldies
on fire, the would-be sister, Glenda, I inhabit,
drives a transformed hearse inside America
all night. Craving breast milk cut with booze,
seduced, come dawn, by Last Chance Supper Hut,
she catches Death (dressed as a stranger
in a red and white checked shirt) paying
attention: I'd got her self large
in pink panties. Our brother's body, rubbing
up a lit flashlight under
his own chin, bones jutting fierce over his glowing
dents of cheeks, black sockets blind, the tips
of his red curls torched devilish
from down below, our ghostly brother, just
last summer, trembled
in her ribcage, the one gray body
of starved pigeons closing in
across Trafalgar Square. Our father faked
flirty accents with the Bobbies. Every night,
candlelight laughing on the white walls
of rented rooms, our father failed
at pounding his wife's shadow
into a new shape. Kicked out from the nest
of her green sheets, a wild
turkey's skull drops, sharp
and hollow, through my fumble, and rolls
down to the slit foot
of the shut door, the fluorescent
milk-white other slicing
in. The halls of heaven must be quiet, and pure cold.
No turning knob. No flowered Oz. No hope of God.

In Heavy Fog Outside Bishopville, South Carolina

DAVID STARKEY

I held the slippery secret of life
between my thumb and forefinger.

Don't ask me now what the secret was;
it shot too quick back into the swamp

and stands of pine. I only know
it had to do with the beauty of light suffused

in unexpected ways, with the power of the imagination
to people empty space,

with Heaven and Earth
and the gap between.

Oh, I can't say I was happy
those few strange moments on the Interstate.

But I know I was at peace.

Underwater

HEATHER SELLERS

Well, we are underwater here and I am
worried, my mother says on the phone
from Florida. How're your dogs?
How are your headaches? she asks me and
then she says Let me call you back, your
phone bills are going to be astronomical.

Then there is long depression.
There are the dogs, rolling in
poop as frequently as possible.
Then there's the sun's going
out one day, which consoles me
over dying, a little but not much.

My sister is in the hospital, receiving
electroconvulsive therapy. The shocking gives
her headaches that make her crazy. Mother
says I don't mean to be rude here, but I can't
be two places at once. You're with her, right?
I'm in a flood here of Biblical dimensions!

The quark guy on the radio is interested in what
everybody else is doing. In his studio in Santa Fe, he sees no
difference between the stock market and the immune
system. Rich is healthy. You're asking me How
are the dogs doing? Marking their territory.
Suggesting fear and worry. Crumpling.

You can't be two places at once? You are always at least
two places at once. That is alive person. That is called The Walking
Dead. The problem is this: those of us who are paying
attention, I mean really paying attention, we are millions of places
at a time. It's hard, it's down to this — in a deep dark blue warm sea we are
    just one eye on the tiniest of the peculiar glowing fish.

Cross-Cultural Genres

WENDY BISHOP

Here is an Eskimo ABC book. Here is Tununak graveyard, filled with snow, blown in shapes of animals moving just beneath the cold skin. Picket fence pierces like spearheads, herds life toward an orthodox cross.

Houses in a white-on-white landscape sit like square ships, antennae pointed toward outer space which doesn't exist in a land where "they deny planning." The universe exists, yet an elder's narrative seems, unfairly, a mouthful of glottal stops, remolding my conception of story — plot, tension, dramatic moment — I drift and slip into another meaning system with Adam Fisher, nasal laugh and nasal laugh and nasal laugh.

We have no real patience for stories. We who "always talk about what's going to happen later" never stop to examine what is. She's young — just started having periods. Shimmies skinny slim hips, squeezes them into comfortable straight Wranglers, walks different but like her older brother, calls electricity to the ends of crackling black hair that she smoothes in hanks.

Silence is built into the land, pale off-tan grass, gathered Sundays after the traveling priest moves out of the village on a snow machine. Machine sputters and shrives silence then engulfs the Bering Sea while Adam Fisher tells a story, nasal laugh and nasal laugh and nasal laugh.

Things with hair stand out: musk ox, seal, men, women. Perspective is plotted by color of bronze skin and enlivened faces against muted palate of weathered buildings, steam of sweat houses, undergreen of tundra, far gray of airplane shadow.

"They are too indirect, too inexplicit. They don't make sense. They just leave without saying anything." In the Tununak graveyard, snow shifts shapes, graves fill, grass bows down, As Bs Cs tussle with sea wind. They leave, they leave without saying anything.

Seizure

MICHELE WOLF

You spoke in a language only you could imagine
Or fathom: "I have to go blankus the eptor" —
Your singsong cadence and syntax making sense.
So this was what it meant, talking in tongues.
You hadn't forewarned me, the evening
Of our first coupling, that this sometimes happens
In your sleep. You awoke with a growl, unable
To hear or see, your whole body stiffened,
Shaking as if invaders had fixed on
Evicting you from your skin, gasping
As if in the last tremors of life.
I thought I had lost you.
Yet soon you emerged from this darkness,
Consumed by a foreign speech. When you finally
Awakened, every muscle sore, exhausted,
You stammered, "I'm sorry," a rush of soft sounds
Echoing, trailing off. Profoundly embarrassed,
You lacked any recollection of what had passed.
Seizure: Needing sleep, you drifted off,
Holding me to you. I didn't dream that night,
In some strange tongue or any other.
Over the distance, I rested
The flesh of me next to the field of you,
The entire hidden field, sparking and rumbling.

Shoyn Fergéssin: "I've Forgotten" in Yiddish

ALBERT GOLDBARTH

But now it's the Yiddish itself I'm forgetting;
it's back on the wharf, in a grimed-over jar
we can barely see into. What's this: is it a cameo brooch,
the bride's profile eaten-at by pickle-brine; or
is it a slice of radish? This is a tooth,
yes? We can turn that jar in the sun all day and
not be able to read it. There's a label, with a name
in black script dancing just beyond arm's reach.

———

A woman is weeping. What did he *do*? he asks
the noncommittal stars, the dark and rhythmic water,
even the slimy pilings. This is a wharf,
in summer. He tells her a joke, not that
it does much good. This is my grandfather,
Louie (in English). This is my grandmother, *Rosie*.
1912. They're in each other's arms again by morning
and don't need to say a word.

———

We'll find them, like ancient coins or arrowheads.
Now they can only be approximate. Here, washed up
on the beach: a few maxims, song titles, even that joke.
It goes: " 'You're a Jew, how come you have a name
like Sean Ferguson?' He says, 'I was so frightened
when we landed at Ellis Island that I couldn't remember
anything for a minute. So that's what I said. They asked me
my name and I said *I've forgotten*.' "

Prodigal

PETER COOLEY

You had walked out, carrying the rain
lightly over your shoulder
on this path you cut through coming home;
you had taken rocks, the ground itself
& wiped your name from them:
holystone, you said, *holystone,*
rhyming the echo, the echo, the echo.

You had called yourself the last star
in your father's eyes, the bright one
nobody could put out. You stood
where the sky stopped turning forever
whenever you caught his stare.
Then your brother found you, narrowed,
& shot up, a sleek, expensive tree

twining his roots under the house.
Just to think of it you shuddered
packing up your room while mother
went about the business of mothers
with your brother's limbs circling your father
till you stood mute at the door.
But already you were somebody else

suffering the cage, the rich, stiff smell
of yourself, your fights nightly
& the ditches of women, that molten lead
every sky turned toward without a word —
so now tonight the branches thicken, bristling
a whole past you push back at the gate
making your return absurdly difficult,

& vines crawl underfoot reminding you
how deep your leaving was, and snakes
rise at either side while you begin to sing
goodbye, goodbye, this time without words
for the house, his now, standing in the moon
& your brother's face catching the light
erect, lifting how far it took you to get here.

Barbie, Madame Alexander, Bronislawa Wajs

VIVIAN SHIPLEY

I told Jerzy Ficowski if you print my songs in Problemy,
my people will be naked, I will be skinned alive. Desperate
to reclaim my ideas, my words, I rushed to Warsaw, begged

the Polish Writer's Union to intervene. At the publishing house,
no one understood me. I went home, burned all of my work,
three hundred poems. Ficowski used my real name, Bronislawa

Wajs, even though I'm known by my gypsy name, Papusza
which translates to doll. That did not matter to the Baro Shero,
I was magerdi, defiled. Punishment was irreversible: exclusion.

It's raining again, a cold prickly rain that makes the window
look like a Spielberg effect on TV. If only my memories could
dissolve one luminous dot at a time but the mud season has

begun with snowmelt. The mantle of the earth is mush, sucking
off my boots when I try to walk away. Water stains, etching
the ceiling like an antique map of my heart. Thirty-four years,

alone, shunned by nieces, nephews, unknown to their children,
I'm discarded, mute as my name, Doll. My family's voice, I still
hear it in my voice which is my mother's, my father's voice.

The older I have gotten, the more I recall although I will allow
no one to listen to my poems or songs. Harpists, my people
hauled great stringed instruments upright as if they were sails

on wagons carting us from northern Lithuania to eastern Tatras.
If we stopped for more than a day, I'd steal a chicken, take it
to another villager to exchange for reading and writing lessons.

Another chicken or two, I got a book or paper. When my father
or brothers caught me, I was beaten, my books, poems buried.
Married at fifteen to Dionizy Wajs, revered as a harpist but old,

I had a work station in a courtyard corner, a tin tub on wood.
Pour in boiling water: rub, rub, rub. The rhythm in my poems
was born in blankets and rugs, the words in my unhappiness.

I was the youngest wife, a *boria*, who got up before everything
even the *khaxni*, the hens. In the sooty light, I followed the rules:
move in silence, collect wood, build the fire, heat water, coffee,

do not speak to a man in the morning before he washes his face.
All day I talked about sheep parts: brains, balls, guts, organs,
glands, skinned heads, joints. I would pinch other girls' breasts

in greeting, in play. None of my hard work was mentioned when
I was pronounced *magerdi* and then banished from the *kumpani*.
The charges spoken were that I had no children, that I invented

long ballads to lament being poor, impossible love, rootlessness,
lost freedom and the *lungo drom*, or long road. A gypsy, I had
ou topos, no place to dream about, no homeland to yearn for.

Tinsmiths, blacksmiths but no Romulus and Remus, no Aeneas
wandering to do battle for me. No anthem or Holocaust memorial
because no names were recorded. Papusza, I sang my poems

in Romani called the cant of thieves, argot of liars, but changing
words meant survival depending on secret laws that could never
be written in order to hide the past, to make a hedge to protect us

from the *gadje*, the non-Gypsies. I blackened pages with elegies
for our nomadic life spread out like skeletons of carp wrapped
in a map of Europe. For thirty-four years, I have hidden my face,

afraid to thumb books or open newspapers, see Ficowski's face
who'll ask *So now where is your poetry?* Silenced by exclusion,
living in a well, no voice called down, Papusza. Romani echoes.

Marime, Magerdi is still warm as the spot where Baro Shero
touched the finger I had used to write down our gypsy songs.
Sentient, my hands kept memory, could not let go, could not ball

to a fist, penetrate the hedge. Papusza will be closed over; *death
date unknown* will be my final sentence. I told Jerzy Ficowski
if you print my songs in *Problemy,* I will be skinned alive, my

people will be naked. My words did not even light a tiny flicker,
but mouth to my ear, voices I remember that will be buried with
me have more than the sound of one lifetime, more than my own.

American Suite for a Lost Daughter

JACK RIDL

I am the last greylag on the left side of the V.

I am the amen in the prayer you never say.

I can bring some stones to you, to the place
you left as a child, the place where the wolves
came to drink and watch you. They watched
you through eyes set deep in the land.

Here you wait, while the dark moon
keeps to its path and the owl watches
the rabbit sit beneath the net of hollow stars.

Christ did not read palms; his lonely
eyes saw the way the lightning grazed
the sky and shot the mind full of questions.
His heart was the color of the center of a tangerine.
His hands lived alone.

Somewhere in any city is a late night
disc jockey looking out the window
to his left, thinking about the bills
he pays, the children he cannot raise,
the wife he tries to love because he wants
to love her and this madness we call
music as it moves out and into the dark air.

You came through a tunnel that began
in the mind's assent to the ancient gnaw.
Your walk has grown from the terrible
chance. Your voice rises and adds its

being to the winds, to that of the piano
and machine gun, the cruel demand and
the long withdrawing sigh of your strange question.

I try to dream your dreams — to let
my mind enter yours and live the intrusions
that keep you from everything you should have.
I find the song we all sing.

I am thinking again of distances.

Your brother came alone
amidst the streaks of sun.
He tosses balls; he somersaults.
You were once so little you
could become an arch; bent
backwards you could walk
around your yard. You could
sit, spread your legs, lean
your forehead into the cool summer grass.

Brahms on the stereo.
You on your bicycle.

I knew your great-uncle Mac.
He would always hold the chair
for Aunt Fan. He loved raking leaves.
Some days I think of all the dead
you can never know. Some days they
are a cloud moving over your own roof.

When you were seven, I suddenly
became "Dad." I wondered
if I should tell you then how far
I was from being a father.

In our herb garden grow thyme,
marjoram, rosemary, lemon balm,
and a weed we named white whisper.

The night, like an idiot savant, does
over and over its one miraculous task.

I want us to be important
for no reason at all.

Then I think of you, broken
and stunned, sitting alone, your
life taken and the only thing left
whatever clings to your mind,
you near death wondering still
why this terrible life had to be
lived within.

I would pray for your life if I could.

Yesterday, as two planes collided
and fell across several southern
California homes, bodies flung
through the cool breeze and slammed
into the ground I thought of the wound
between us, how it will never heal, how
impossible it has become to sense
or gauge the pain that hurls itself
across this age of circumstances no one
can recover from. Prayer. Prayer.
If none of this can bring a god to
end it all, then . . . I remember
the nights we walked and tried
to see only the stars.

Scoured

DAVID STARKEY

My two daughters chase each other
in the laundromat, past the banks
of Speedqueens, between
the industrial Wash-o-matics.
They dart after loose buttons
and puffs of lint, gifts
they bring to me.

        Christ!
A hundred dollars for a used machine
and I can't come up with it.
God's benediction upon these children,
but I wish they would vanish.
I want the power to leave
at a moment's notice, the power
to tear down every single wall in my house.

I want to be as clean as fresh laundry.
I want a shell
that's hard and whorled so deep
I cannot hear the beat
and drum of poverty
thumping
like a clump of wet clothes in a dryer:
I *want*, I *want*.

I have nothing at all to give.

The Estrangement of Luis Morone

STUART DYBEK

Luis Morone
cuts adrift

sinks flies
flickers out

it's dark
in his room

they screw
in a bulb

find rags
on hangers

resembling
his body

a pin-up
with a thumbtack
stigmata

crucifix
with a snapped
G string

rat trap
abandoned

mirror abandoned
to the blued
wind of a muzzle

desire abandoned
anger abandoned

birth death
abandoned abandoned

cortege of roaches
carting off crumbs

in other words
nothing

much changed
by his absence

loans outstanding
love

and other debts
still outstanding

Don't worry kids
you still have
twelve uncles

and children are born
to mourn their lost fathers

Don't worry Mother
you aren't blind
nobody sees him

For the Sake of Tiger Lilies

C. DALE YOUNG

In a clearing, in a swell of grasses
thick with greens and yellows, he cannot forget
the ocean miles below the jagged rift,

the afternoons not laden with orchids,
afternoons not brilliant, overwhelmed
by the croton leaves inflamed with sunlight.

Papa glares at me, his voice tremulous:
"The day is underneath the day —
there is too much freewheeling,

too much banter for the sake of posture,
for the sake of tiger lilies
drooping their speckled orange heads.

The ocean is always waiting, Son.
An islander is never far from it,
always the sound, always the salt licking the air."

Lamentation Canzone

SEAN THOMAS DOUGHERTY
— *for Garry Victorin, 1964–83*

Why after so much breath
do you return to me from the body, the city
has kept you silent for so long, the breath
of your face as you slept that night, drunk on the
    lawn, breath
of running through the playgrounds, sound of a
    dead
basketball thudding against the asphalt, winter
    breath
I try to capture with my hands, breath
that rises white as moonlight, the clock
above your bed froze at 11:10, the clock
that rings downtown as we walked from work,
    breath
of dust from the newspaper plant, child-
-hood I try to hold, watch it wisp — child

I carry in my hands, my son crying at night, *child*
you will never caress, never let your breath
touch his gentle hands — *what of the children*
you would have had, the woman whose child
you would have held, wiped the fevered forehead,
    city
of dead end streets, bad brakes and bad checks, *a*
    child
floats on a sea of glass, glass child
that splinters in my hands, dead
child with eyes of green, water of the dead
is the deepest river, the Ferryman calls, *child*
that sleeps in the breath of wind, hear the clock
downtown strike twice for two, it is the clock

that wakes me from sleep, calluses on my hands,
    clock
above your station at work, you told me you wanted
    a child
before you turned twenty, someone to teach you to
    live against the clocks
that controlled our lives — *let the wind blow her*
    black hair, clocks
we spit against, working those nights, loading the
    trucks, breath
white as winter, snow on the docks, *the clock*
would strike one and we'd walk home from the third
    shift, clock
in the hallway of your building — the city
was made of sleep those nights the snow fell, city
along the Merrimack River, textile city, clock
city, *city made of timecards and clocks*, broken
    threads the dead
wove into textiles, Pandora sweaters, dresses, dead

that spoke to us alone at night along the river, the
    ghosts of the dead
who walked to work, swinging their pails — your
    mother during the day, the clock
that woke her, she gathered her beaded bag and
    walked to the plant, *dead*
tired she dragged herself home, baked fish and rice
    for your old man, *dead*
to the world, this world, but in the evening *her*
    hands turned to prayers, child
she saw you as, altar boy, the good child, the child
    with the strong voice, dead
child, *deadchilddeadchilddeadchild* the dead
are those whose eyes cannot stare, breath

I want to weave in air, breath
I tried to hold, the threads, *the threads*, wake the
    dead
this night, call them to hold the living, offer them
    the keys to this city,
this city, this city whose name is nothing, nowhere.
    Somewhere in this city

there is snow being shoveled, *there is the long sob
    of a sick child*, this fragrant city
of too much musk in dead-end bars, men who
    worked the machines gone dead
to Mexico, *Dia de Muerte, Ciudad de Muerte*, city
    of Allied Chemical, Steel, polluted city
where Iroquois once built longhouses, spiraling
    smoke, city you have never seen, *my walled
    city*
since I moved away, left your body beneath the
    grass, your little brothers all grown, *the clock
never stops ticking*, my hand is on my chest, *my
    brother* this is another city
far from the river where we walked at night,
    skipped stones along the millyard tracks, city
of old bridges, red brick and broken glass, city that
    a child
sleeps in, where we slept, where you grew up tall
    far from Haiti, child
of sugarcane and French, the sepia'd photos of
    Port Au Prince, that city
where your father showed you shells, taught you
    Patois, breath
of rum on his face, *I can't even remember his name* —
    breath

is something we lose I found out as I watched you
    fade, breath

is something we can never hold, we were never
   children
I sometimes think. Walled city of my heart: I try
   to set the clock,
the hands that spin, with each new spin the dead
are borne along the deepest river. Just beyond
   my grasp is the suburb of your new city.

On Being Told I Don't Speak Like a Black Person

ALLISON JOSEPH

Emphasize the "h," you hignorant ass,
was what my mother was told
when colonial-minded teachers
slapped her open palm with a ruler
in that Jamaican schoolroom.
Trained in England, they tried
to force their pupils to speak
like Eliza Doolittle after
her transformation, fancying themselves
British as Henry Higgins,
despite dark, sun-ripened skin.
Mother never lost her accent,
though, the music of her voice
charming everyone, an infectious lilt
I can imitate, not duplicate.
No one in the States told her
to eliminate the accent,
my high school friends adoring
the way her voice would lift
when she called me to the phone,
A-ll-i-son, it's friend Cathy.
Why don't you sound like her?,
they'd ask. I didn't sound
like anyone or anything,
no grating New Yorker nasality,
no fastidious British mannerisms
like the ones my father affected
when he wanted to sell someone
something. And I didn't sound
like a Black American,
college acquaintances observed,

sure they knew what a black person
was supposed to sound like.
Was I supposed to sound lazy,
dropping syllables here, there,
not finishing words but
slurring the final letter so that
each sentence joined the next,
sliding past the listener?
Were certain words off limits,
too erudite, too scholarly
for someone with a natural tan?
I asked what they meant,
and they stuttered, blushed,
said you know, Black English,
applying what they'd learned
from that semester's text.
Does everyone in your family
speak alike?, I'd question,
and they'd say don't take this the
wrong way, nothing personal.

Now I realize there's nothing
more personal than speech,
that I don't have to defend
how I speak, how any person,
black, white, chooses to speak.
Let us speak. Let us talk
with the sounds of our mothers
and fathers still reverberating
in our minds, wherever our mothers
or fathers come from:
Arkansas, Belize, Alabama,
Brazil, Aruba, Arizona.
Let us simply speak
to one another,

listen and prize the inflections,
differences, never assuming
how any person will sound
until her mouth opens,
until his mouth opens,
greetings familiar
in any language.

El Balserito

CAMPBELL MCGRATH

Because my Spanish is chips-and-salsa simple, and I am desirous of improving upon it, and delighted whenever I can puzzle out on my own some new word or phrase, I am listening in on the conversation of the two Cuban men next to me at the counter of the plumbing supply store in Little Haiti, and when I hear the word *balserito* I recognize this to be a diminutive of *balsero*, "the rafter," that symbol of the Cuban-American experience, those cast ashore on scrapwood rafts emblematic of an entire community's exile, and when the one man goes out to his truck and comes back with a little plastic dashboard toy of Goofy and another Disney character floating in an inner tube, and the other man, laughing and smiling at the joke asks, *Quien es el otro?*, pointing at the smaller figure, I know that this is Max, Goofy's son, because we have just taken Sam to see *A Goofy Movie*, a story of father-son bonding in the cartoon universe, a universe in many ways more familiar to me than this one, though of course I say nothing to the men, not wanting to admit I have been eavesdropping, or betray my linguistic insufficiency, the degree to which I am an outsider here, in Miami, a place unlike any other I have known, a city we have fixed upon like Rust Belt refugees eager to buy a little piece of the sunshine, to mortgage a corner of the American Dream, where already Sam has begun to master the local customs, youngest and most flexible, first to make landfall, betraying the generational nature of acculturation the way the poems of my students at the state university do, caught between past and present worlds, transplanted parents looking back to Havana while the children are native grown, rooted to the soil, though the roots of *las palmas* are notoriously shallow, hence their propensity to topple in a hurricane, tropical storm, even the steady winter tradewind bearing its flotilla of makeshift sails across the Straits of Florida, so many this season that some mornings, jogging along the boardwalk in the shadow of the luxury hotels, I have come upon three rafts washed up in a single mile of beach, ragged planks and styrofoam and chicken wire, filthy and abandoned but curiously empowered, endowed with a violent, residual energy, like shotgun casings in a field of corn stubble or the ruptured jelly of turtle eggs among mangroves, chrysalides discarded as the cost of the journey, shells of arrival, shells of departure.

Ninety-one in the Shade

ROBERT DANA

It's not enough to be good . . .
— James Baldwin

1

It's always the same

These swelters of brick or boards
The humid tons of air
Metallic breath of ancient drains

In the kitchen
flies cruise the centuries of unwashed dishes
Cops cruise the streets

Your third floor Thirties apartment
taken for space and sleeping porches
decays visibly month by month

But your green plants thrive
in this north light

And the moon of your white face
is still beautiful

2

After supper
we walk to the bakery
for rolls and black strong bread

or to the laundromat
where our colors gasp and collapse like
television
in the rented glass
of washer doors

The neighborhood
sweats on its dark stoops

Teasing
or pussy-maddened
or weirdo delinquent junkies on a glassy high

In the occasional swing
of headlights
the features of an obscene photograph

where feeling
is the jagged edge of thought

the body
all that keeps us alive

3

Dead black
of morning

And we wake
to the rich burn of ozone
and the distant low batteries of thunder

Lightning
freaks the roaches
from the bedroom floor

I tell you
how sometimes I imagine myself
an enemy soldier

Summer storms
as artillery shelling the city

Naked on the bed

we talk about
whether you think of yourself
as beautiful

about your girlhood

your older sister
who is unhappy

The rain has begun to fall

Clicking in the leaves
beside the window

Puddling the rutted alleys

Then
whistling through the screens
scouring the sills

it monsoons
into the empty streets

cold and foot-wringing

until our windows blur
like the stunned windows in a dream

the endless succession of rented rooms
in which nobody lives

4

Along del Mar
seven days a week

the jag of gas-blue ghost-green letters
and girls

hot-nippled in neon
sizzling on then off then on

Spelling it out

Strain your gut
in the sheep-kill forever

You will never
own a house on the water

Or under the green trees
where time passes quickly

and the wings of butterflies
are dusted a delicate blue

5

Our last morning together
you sit on the edge of the bed
stroking a vein in your thigh

Your hair
smells of coffee and eggs

If I kiss you
you will cry

In a vacant lot
where the baked earth blinks with the mercy
of broken glass

a small black boy
tries to get his tailless kite
to fly

The three of us
tie the rag of my handkerchief to it

And watch it
haul at its saddle-string

tugging the live sail of its colors up
into the hot gust

like a word remembered

that we do not say

35-mm Clips

RICHARD BLANCO

Here is my past. I'm able to remember none of it,
memories of those years are only what I accept
as true from grainy scenes thrown on a wall:
a living roomful lit-up with rummed laughter
and relatives dancing for the camera to the birth
of Jesus on *Noche Buena*, the "Good Night,"
or close-up faces huddled over birthday candles
as I turned two — is that me refusing a smile or
my mother's hand down Broadway at midday
(when was I ever so unbound, so endless)?

A family history recorded by reactions of light
that is either blaring or not enough for the lens,
and so the film is either a wash of diluted color
or saturated with silhouettes of shifting poses.
For all of 1971 my brother bounces a rubber ball
against a graffiti wall, oblivious to the writing,
while *Abuelo* looks on (his hair once black?),
his *tabaco* a chimney trailed by dreamy smoke
that cuts to scenes of Niagara Falls — nothing
but the deluge, the deluge, and then the ocean
at Miami Beach, waves dismantling at the feet
of my aging aunts half-dressed, half-beautiful
walking a lucid shore (half of them gone now).

Every step quickened to the speed of the film,
and every move silent save the reeling and hum
of the projector projecting wordless images
trying to convince me that I remember all this,
that I remember you *Papá*, on Riverside Drive
smoking, pretending not to be filmed, focused

on an imaginary point across the Hudson gray.
In the distance, suspended above your head,
the George Washington Bridge stands a solid
blur of steel and concrete, now I'm guessing
where it begins, where it ends; I'm guessing
at the places you meant to go, all you left
behind, days waited too long to set aside,
all you meant to say, how you might say it
in this silent film, your back to the camera.

The End of Soup Kitchens

MARK TAKSA

You put your money on the pavement
and I teach you poker. Your future is in my pocket.
I whisper that a tulip is luck when you are cold on asphalt.
My blue lips testify that you can't beat the shuffle
unless you see that purple bulb
sprouting from the steamy pavement.

You follow me into the soup kitchen.
Paying my bills and joking about a loser
whose best poker is without cards, I refuse
to know you in the chow line
where lunch is grass without rain.
You call me an empty refrigerator.

Your life is a jacket of snow
and you cannot tear it off. You are sticking a pole,
gum at its end, through metal grating in steamy pavement.
You fish for coins theater lovers lost.

Now that you are naked in ice,
a quarter gummed to a stick is a tulip. You pull up the stick,
cover your wilting wealth with your torso;
in this necessary instant, the sun is a torch
over anything that blocks its light.

You put your tulip into your cap.
In the hunger where a cop arrests anyone
catching a pavement philosophy
and where, if you listen, wind gets louder in barbed wire,
the flower grows over the soup kitchen

and you and the other bums play catch
and the last person to hold the tulip
declares the end of soup kitchens.

Poem at an Unmarked Grave

JUDITH VOLLMER

Your grave is untouched by flowers
I might have brought.
You left me this fierce love of spaces.
My newest memorial to you
is a meadow garden holding stones
of many shapes: mushroom, serpent,
loaf of bread. You enter through the East
and spiral through it
till you come to two log chairs.
It's stunning
the way wind through the pines
still can't make the sound of your voice.

"Everyplace is like everyplace," you'd laugh
those nights we stayed enchanted
till dawn at your drafting table smoking
and drawing boulevards & libraries.
Your front windows above the shining intersections
were the eyes I used: the body
of Pittsburgh curved under snow,
sculpted finally into our dreams of it, whole,
the public domain of the universities & factories
met the sturdy chimneys & streets of our privacy.
We were twenty and lived inside Emerson's miracle:
a college education is a room with a fire
inside a strange city.

Portrait of a Couple at Century's End

SHEROD SANTOS

Impatient for home,
the after-work traffic fanning out along
the wet streets, a jagged sound,
like huge sheets of construction paper torn
their length, and through

the walls, the shudder
of the furnace, as though a hundred thousand
bottle-flies were trapped between
the clapboards and the plaster. A gentler
rain blows across

the TV screen, where
a CNN foreign correspondent tells
how a single Serb mortar shell
just leveled the crowded terrace of a
Tuzla café.

The darker crimes are
faceless in that lidless, immemorial
eye (*a world outside, a world
within*), so summer's what they talk about,
the meal, their work,

and how they quarreled
one night in Iowa. The buried longings
such memories stir. And yet,
in what they can't express they remind us
of something too,

of something we've felt
settle on our lives, in shadow-life of ours.
So forget for a moment
the future of their monogamous hearts,
forget the rain,

the traffic, the boot-
soles pressed forever in our century's mud,
for it's all there, whatever
they'd say, the industry of pain, the Ho-
ly Spirit of

everything that's been
taken away, it's all there in the burnt match-
head preserved into amber
by a beeswax candle pooling beside
their dinnerware.

Towns

ANGELA BALL

There are no sagas — only trees now, animals, engines: There's that.
— William Carlos Williams, Notes in Diary Form, 1927

Somewhere in midcentury
things spread out, scattered
and came close at the same time —
distances suddenly efficient,
flying by night.

What about the little towns
so full of themselves once?

The people — this is crucial —
don't think of themselves as alive
in the center of things.
Potential is out of the question,
although there is a new planet,
atomic, maybe, with night clouds
of orange. When it first came
it was out of context, cowed
looking: now it's the town.

Americans are good at movie sets:
they like the raw, the provisional.
The pioneers (some of them
our father's fathers — that recent!)
lined up their best chairs in front of the house
to sit and be photographed.
Then people posed with their cars, machines
with fat curves, wheels set wide.
Didn't know yet that moving
would take power, would be the one
bright life.

I don't think it's the change itself
that's so frightening, but the vacancy
left behind it. I heard of a faraway
ancient village, a conversation
between a Buddhist and a feldspar man
who said, "If we take this mineral,
it will help your village." The Buddhist
replied, "Yes. But our village
will not be here."

Four Clouds Like the Irish in Memory

CAMPBELL MCGRATH

First memory of school: sitting in the grass beneath a blossoming dogwood
tree while the teacher explains how to write a poem.

Boisterous sun, orbital crab apples, isn't the springtime beautiful? What do
the clouds look like? Butterfly, banana split, polar bear, clown. What does
the dogwood look like, its bracts and tiers and white cascades of flowers?
Snowflakes. A birthday cake. Good, good. Like going to New York for the
holidays, like heaven or the George Washington Bridge at night, its titanium
spans and whirligigs, garlands of popcorn, garlands of cranberries, baked ham
and my grandfather's accordion, my mother and her sisters trying out their old
Shirley Temple routines amidst an Irish stew of relatives and well-wishers
immersed for the day in the nostalgic mist and manners of the old sod.

Shamrock, whiskey bottle, subway train, diaspora.

One year my grandfather drove with us back to Washington after Christmas.
I remember him chiefly for that matchless accordion, the hats and boats he
made from newspaper, the senility that claimed him like an early snowfall —

as I remember my father's father for the crafty wooden puzzles he assembled
at the kitchen table with a box of Ritz crackers and quart of Rheingold beer —

but this was my mother's father, a countryman from Donegal, famous for long
strolls in Riverside Park collecting weeds for home remedies, for walking the
bridge to save a penny on a pack of cigarettes. He worked forty years as a ticket
taker in the subway, pent too long 'mid cloisters dim, and somewhere in
southern New Jersey, in the backseat of the station wagon looking out past
the turnpike, he said, in his thick brogue, to no one in particular, *goodness.*

I had no idea there were such great forests left.

A Northern Darkness

DIXIE PARTRIDGE

In it we are seers with no eyes.
— Gretel Ehrlich

Winds die and shadows wrap us
in trunks of trees. We anticipate silence
with last light from the south,
the day-moon enlarging
northwest in fir.

A place like this long ago
I first heard the word *wild*
in *bewilder: be wild*
be wilder, be wilderness. . . .

My father said *camp*
where you can hear water,
and I wish for that inkling
of moving on while everything stands
in a trance under night.
With the deepening around our lantern,
thought turns basic: darkness, light;
matter and spirit; earth

and the sky . . . salted with stars.
The faint hymn of our breath
pales visibly.

III. Invocations

Absence

PETER MEINKE

Some people like broken glass
are known by absence:
she's one of those students
who never goes to class

like unpublished scribblers
known for what
they might have done if not
for the job and the little nibblers

unvoiced echoes
of an agonized shout
someone thinks about
shouting but never does

as with a childless marriage
a couple's bind
is negatively defined
like a horseless carriage

as with an air of distraction
twiddling the doorknob
the man from Porlock
made a great subtraction

One can get further away
from life than one might imagine
like a would-be has-been
not catching on in papier-mâché

or a man (say) working in rhyme
his insides much
out of touch
with the times

For Someone Considering Death

LOLA HASKINS

I told you.
Life is one big Hanon
up and down the piano,
ten fingers skipping over each other
in every conceivable way,
two hands getting stronger.

And sure,
the notes are the same for everyone,
but you can choose to whisper or shout,
to fade or grow.
And haven't you noticed that some people's hands sing,
but others are midwestern on the keys,
each crescendo a secretarial swell.

Think about this.
How can you dream to play the Pathétique,
how can the moment come to truly look
into someone's eyes
and say, *the hell with everything, I love you,*
when you haven't done your time,
hour after hour, year after year,
in that small, closed room.

Dwarf with Violin, Government Center Station

STANLEY PLUMLY

The long-distance connections fade and rectify
like wind tracking the filaments of wire
through the echo of tunnel,
the emptiness and silence pushed on up
ahead of the great green toy trains rattling
and grinding to their stops, so that the notes
have to rise even higher, toward ignition,
as electric as the switches, at a line
above the static, except they don't.
They coil and ravel out like thought.

The violin is almost the size
of the man, and graduates the longer
it is listened to, as the woman in
blankets will hear it whole through the heroin
and chill. It is a moment meant to
make us forget the moment, since the soul
wants a pastoral, a green tree on a hill:
it will close its eyes in the cave of winds
and pick the human sound, however flawed;
in the deathless weather of the understructure,

among the dead who travel underground,
it will be appalled, appeased, and then
the longing, then the coming up for air
to a sort of spring in winter, early
blossoming, yellow in the aisles around
the Common, snow-scar and construction.
The friend I saw broken, leaning against
a building, was no one I knew. I had a noise
like music in my head. Everything took heart.
Everything looked alive as if forgotten.

Postcards to Columbus

SHERMAN ALEXIE

Beginning at the front door of the White House, travel west
for 500 years, pass through small towns and house fires, ignore
hitchhikers and stranded motorists, until you find yourself
back at the beginning of this journey, this history and country

folded over itself like a Möbius strip. Christopher Columbus
where have you been? Lost between Laramie and San Francisco
or in the reservation HUD house, building a better mousetrap?
Seymour saw you shooting free throws behind the Tribal School

in a thunderstorm. Didn't you know lightning strikes the earth
800 times a second? But, Columbus, how could you ever imagine
how often our lives could change? *Electricity is lightning pretending
to be permanent* and when the Indian child pushes the paper clip

into the electrical outlet, it's applied science, insane economics
of supply and demand, the completion of a 20th-century circuit.
Christopher Columbus, you are the most successful real estate agent
who ever lived, sold acres and acres of myth, a house built on stilts

above the river salmon travel by genetic memory. Beneath the burden
of 15,000 years, my tribe celebrated this country's 200th birthday
by refusing to speak English and we'll honor the 500th anniversary
of your invasion, Columbus, by driving blindfolded cross-country

naming the first tree we destroy *America*. We'll make the first guardrail
we crash through our national symbol. Our flag will be a white sheet
stained with blood and piss. Columbus, can you hear me over the white noise
of your television set? Can you hear ghosts of drums approaching?

Postmodernism

DAVID BAKER

The scene you loathe, the sheer fervor, the speed
     of the dangerous cabs — the city street
in oil, in spray when they pass, and the white
     exhaustion of the passersby like clouds.

You've been fired or you're on your way to work.
     If you're reading this it doesn't matter.
What matters is you're wet, and hurrying
     or hungry, or not, or in no hurry

whatsoever. It's almost this easy.
     When you duck inside the café doorway,
the body smell of the animal stone,
     to find a little shelter — there's your face

like a face in the plate-glass sheet and door.
     There's the wealthy hungry, seated inside.
On the other side, past the entrance, the rained-
     out passageway of air and stone, bombed-out

crapped-out building in a husk of smoke, there's
     the junkie, coughing on her cardboard flat.
You see because you see the reflection
     in the big glass, your face like an etching

between them, a breath, or a sudden change
     of venue. It's too convenient, even
for art or argument — are you hungry?
     is she a junkie? — all of you framed for

an instant like a political ad.
     No one is looking at anyone else.
The street surges, it chokes, but you're caught there.
     And now even your pity is worthless.

Survivor's Song

ROBERT PHILLIPS

All my good friends have gone away.
     The boisterous flight of stairs is bare.
There's nothing more I want to say.

First was Jean — she thought she was gay —
     drunk nightly on *vin ordinaire.*
All my good friends have gone away.

And where is Scotty B. today?
     So Southern, so doomed, so savoir-faire?
(There's nothing more I want to say.)

Sweet Hermione was third to stray.
     How her monologues smoked the air!
All my good friends have gone away.

Daniel, our beer-budget gourmet,
     no longer plays the millionaire.
There's nothing more I want to say

Except: My world's papier-mâché.
     I need them all — weren't they aware?
All my good friends have gone away.
There's nothing more I want to say.

Credo

LILACE MELLIN GUIGNARD

I believe in highways,
maps more healing than scripture.
When despair hits head-on
I read out the names of routes that can lead me
past myself, across the Idaho panhandle
following rivers that don't change color or depth
as they cross into the next state.

"Out there," the pavement preaches,
"still exists a land of promises
and all you have to do is drive, children, drive."
I'm proud of the contributions I've made
to all-night-diner ministries.
These are the folks who're there for you,
24 hrs. a day *with coffee,*
strangers who call you honey
and let you sleep in their parking lots
curled into your front seat
under light drifting down with impossible grace
from a blue star cast up as a sign for those
who find it easier to believe in miracles in the dark,
alone, with the time zones blurred,

far away from familiar love
and the well-worn disappointments of home.

Questions for Ecclesiastes

MARK JARMAN

What if on a foggy night in a beachtown, a night when the Pacific leans close
   like the face of a wet cliff, a preacher were called to the house of a suicide,
   a house of strangers, where a child had discharged a rifle through the roof
   of her mouth and the top of her skull?

What if he went to the house where the parents, stunned into plaster statues,
   sat behind their coffee table, and what if he assured them that the sun
   would rise and go down, the wind blow south, then turn north, whirling
   constantly, rivers — even the concrete flume of the great Los Angeles —
   run into the sea, and fourteen-year-old girls would manage to spirit
   themselves out of life, nothing was new under the sun?

What if he said the eye is not satisfied with seeing, nor the ear filled with
   hearing? Would he want to view the bedroom vandalized by self-murder or
   hear the quiet before the tremendous shout of the gun or the people inside
   the shout, shouting or screaming, crying and pounding to get into the
   room, kicking through the hollow-core door and making a new sound
   and becoming a new silence — the silence he entered with his comfort?

What if as comfort he said to the survivors I praise the dead which are dead
   already more than the living, and better is he than both dead and living
   who is not yet alive? What if he folded his hands together and ate his own
   flesh in prayer? For he did pray with them. He asked them, the mother and
   father, if they wished to pray to do so in any way they felt comfortable, and
   the father knelt at the coffee table and the mother turned to squeeze her
   eyes into a corner of the couch, and they prayed by first listening to his
   prayer, then clawing at his measured cadences with tears (the man cried)
   and curses (the woman swore). What if, then, the preacher said be not
   rash with thy mouth and let not thine heart be hasty to utter anything
   before God: for God is in heaven?

What if the parents collected themselves, then, and asked him to follow them
to their daughter's room, and stood at the shattered door, the darkness of
the room beyond, and the father reached in to put his hand on the light
switch and asked if the comforter, the preacher they were meeting for the
first time in their lives, would like to see the aftermath, and instead of
recoiling and apologizing, he said that the dead know not anything for
the memory of them is forgotten? And while standing in the hallway, he
noticed the shag carpet underfoot, like the fur of a cartoon animal, the
sort that requires combing with a plastic rake, leading into the bedroom,
where it would have to be taken up, skinned off the concrete slab of the
floor, and still he said for their love and hatred and envy are now perished,
neither have the dead any more portion for ever in anything that is done
under the sun?

What if as an act of mercy so acute it pierced the preacher's skull and traveled
the length of his spine, the man did not make him regard the memory of
his daughter as it must have filled her room, but guided the wise man, the
comforter, to the front door, with his wife with her arms crossed before
her in that gesture we use to show a stranger to the door, acting out a rite
of closure, compelled to be social, as we try to extricate ourselves by
breaking off the extensions of our bodies, as raccoons gnaw their legs
from traps, turning aside our gaze, letting only the numb tissue of
valedictory speech ease us apart, and the preacher said live joyfully
all the days of the life of thy vanity, for that is thy portion in this life?

They all seem worse than heartless, don't they, these crass and irrelevant
platitudes, albeit stoical and final, oracular, stony, and comfortless? But
they were at the center of that night, even if they were unspoken.

And what if one with only a casual connection to the tragedy remembers
a man, younger than I am today, going out after dinner and returning,
then sitting in the living room, drinking a cup of tea, slowly finding the
strength to say he had visited these grieving strangers and spent some
time with them?

Still that night exists for people I do not know in ways I do not know, though I have tried to imagine them. I remember my father going out and my father coming back. The fog, like the underskin of a broken wave, made a low ceiling that the street lights pierced and illuminated. And God who shall bring every work into judgment, with every secret thing, whether it be good or whether it be evil, who could have shared what He knew with people who needed urgently to hear it, God kept a secret.

No Living in Parked Vehicles

STEVE FAY

— from a street sign in Bayfield, Wisconsin

Only the dead may park, all others
must stay on the move. All drive-ins
are henceforth drive-thrus. Length

and purpose of stopping determines
severity of penalty: to plant a seed
forfeits a hand, to sketch a flower,

an eye. Dumping your ashtray,
however, is everywhere permitted.
The jurisdiction of this statute

extends to all rivers and the Great
Lakes, covers all mineral claims
except strip mines, goes out to sea

three hundred miles, and vertically to
infinity, the North Star having a waiver.
Fishermen must troll, becalmed schooners

will be sunk, innertubes, confiscated.
For your comfort, mobile gas-food-
restroom facilities have been dispatched

to circle at all interstate highway
cloverleaves. Three million square miles
of pavement will shortly be added,

as soon as the apartments come down.
The Director cordially wishes everyone
happy motoring. Now, make it snappy.

Soul

WILLIAM KLOEFKORN
— *for Glenn Bush*

Each time I look at my friend's
   red sunset maple, in season
      or otherwise,

I think of soul, that butterfly
   as yet not pinned to
      anybody's wall,

how that afternoon it left his
   self-destructed flesh
      to find its way

beyond the sealed garage to greener
   pastures. Buy what precisely
      it is, or what it

means, eludes me. Metaphor — soul
   as butterfly — is the best
      that I can do,

connection tenuous and trite, yet
   (forgive me) nonetheless
      unto this moment

sufficient. As a boy my belief
   was this: that with a
      feedsack net

I'd ensnare every butterfly extant
   in Harper County, entrapment
      being that unassailable

proof in the heart of all puddings.
But with each death each
butterfly's soul

escaped in the form of a butterfly,
odorless and very nearly
soundless,

not even the occasional *snick* of a
delicate motor,
missing.

Seven & Seven

PETER MEINKE

Looking back at it now he
can see what a fool he was
but life's not a damn exam

and if being a dunce and
disgrace has dragged him to where
he kneels in this sweltering

sagging house with the shutters
hanging like drunks from a frayed
merry-go-round a pen or

a drink in his hand and her
reading a book while the dogs
circle outside maniacs

running the land no matter
which way we vote he can say
at least we tried and this the

road we took: *twisting below*
the oaks the vines sucking their
trunks where unearthly shadows
mix with the smell of salt and
decay and the swollen threat
of rain warps the cypress boards
and softens the porous ground
until the house tilts like a
monk tipsy beside a stream
that murmurs the drunkard's dream:

Everything can be fixed O
Lord anything can be fixed

Breaking and Entering

WILLIAM BAER

When he was done, he sat in their living room:
as always, he'd made certain they'd be away,
and checked for dogs, alarms, and nosy neighbors,
then glass-cut through a window in the back —
ready with the knife he'd never used
(but would) — and quickly packed her gold and stones,
their small antiques, and the "knock-out" Tiffany lamp —
which these dull bastards certainly didn't deserve.

But he liked their quiet house, just as he'd liked
his parents' best when they were sound asleep,
no nagging, fighting, or banging him about.
Some "sneaks" enjoy the breaking in — "like sex"
they say — while others crave the risks, or just the goods,
but he liked sitting in their living rooms,
until, at last, he'd slit their couches open, and leave.
Too bad. He liked it here; it felt like home.

Joint Venture

MARILYN KRYSL

Shanti can't speak — sweet, flowing
talk, as we know it, not an option.
How came she to be this wail —
she wants something, or does not

want something to happen. Forty
and handsome, a chiseled Lakshmi,
someone I might have fallen
in love with, in situations other than

this one (say swanky dorm, Amherst,
or Smith. Or U.N. delegation,
evidence on Genital Mutilation).
Now everything except food's an invasion.

I talk up the glories of obligatory
bath — "Mother Teresa says you have to" —
ply repertoire of international
motherese: *feel this nice water,*

nothing terrible will happen,
I won't let it — while lorries
galumph past, lumbering the daylights
out of any possibility of beauty,

and Shanti wails. Crows pick walk
through trash, scammers, unabashed,
work the street here in the diesel
diaspora, the day's sweat a caul

I don't want. Sister Luke sweats
with us, but we're without caudle
for the wailing woman, and I'm
coming down with something, feverish

(though who isn't), stomach queasy.
Now Luke throws up her hands, leaves us.
I start the gown, careful to be slow,
left hand through sleeve, over elbow,

maybe this wail's a mantram, Shanti
repeating Hail Marys the only way
she can. I hear it then, the darkened
rhythm rises, turns, swerves upward,

and higher, gliding, now speeding
to the place where the pneumonic wave
breaks, flows out, slides back, recedes
in ocean's turning churn, where,

slowly, it will build again: how
long in its coming, this eloquence
of our brute longing, to my ear —
sung to me here near noon, sun

climbing up through the body, by she
who can't speak or walk out — to me,
who can say what I want exactly
and stroll out, free, but lonely.

Manifesto

MARGOT SCHILPP

Look in the window and extract a name:
Jupiter, melancholy, harp. To love something
you must have considered what it means

to do without. You must have thought
about it — the coefficient of the body
is another body — but do not forget

that there are people who are willing
to staple your palm to your chest.
Know there are places it isn't wise to go.

I know that dying is how we escape
the rest of our lives. I think that trees
send us a message: do not believe

you are lucky. The skins of apples
and the peeler will marry; it's simply
a question of when. Believe

in mourning and carrion birds.
Look how their fleshy treasures
dissolve in the sun before their very eyes.

Begin again if you must: there are ways
to make up for what you have been before,
the dust in the corners that collects you.

Sympathy is overrated. Rethink how lack
becomes everyone's master, drives us
into town and spends our money.

Quiet: the trees are napping.
Water meets itself again.
We reach for the days that precede us

and the world keeps us from knowing
too much. The body loves music,
the abandoned road of it;

each day a peel
lengthens in the shadow of blossoms,
fabric weaves itself into light.

Pay attention to the patterns. They repeat —
terraces erode, groves lie fallow —
order is cognate of joy.

How the Streets in Front of
Kaufmann's Department Store Tell Me I Am Home

RICK CAMPBELL

For years I have been lost. Some nights I have known it
      as I looked out at whatever moon hung
over the wrong trees, watched as too-bright stars
      glimmered in a too-clear sky.
Other nights, sometimes for months or years I have thought
      I was home because the land

had grown familiar, because live oak and loblolly,
      palmetto or magnolia had begun to speak to me
in a tongue I understood. I said I *live here*, and the dark angels
      that flitted about my shoulders, tickling my ears
with their doubts, fell silent in front of the beauty of azaleas,
      the mystery of camellias.

But today I see that I have been gone these many years.
      Three days after snow, little rivers of cinder water
run in the gutters, ridges of plowed snow blacken
      where glass and steel cut off the sun. And
in front of Kaufmann's, in the great windows where mannequins
      show us what we *could* look like

my people — men and women wrapped in gray or brown coats,
      carrying plastic bags, lunch boxes, briefcases,
staring straight ahead or into the past — walk the crowded lunchtime sidewalks.
      We dodge each other, snow and ice and running water.
I'm drawn to the deli across the street, to pastrami and Iron City,
      where everyone eating big sandwiches is big

and thick, and their voices sing *Pittsburgh* when they say *Iron*.
        On the street again in the dark canyon
of Grant Street, I head for the river and Mt. Washington rising
        on its far shore. My eyes climb the tracks
on the incline, its red car inching skyward like a bucket of coal
        winched up a cliff. The Monongahela

is running high and fast, spring snow
        runoff carrying trees, beds, chairs,
and trash toward the Ohio, and I know I am home
        because from here on this bridge
I can see the Allegheny's muddy mountain water
        merge with this gray to birth the Ohio. No headwaters,

no springs rising in a quiet swamp of cattails, the Ohio
        rolls full bore past Neville Island's
abandoned steel plants, past the silence of American Bridge,
        past the gravel slab that was once Jones & Laughlin,
past my bedroom window that once saw the fire, smoke
        and ash of three shifts a day, whole valley working,

living mill lives. From here, because I know that I am home
        I can see twenty-five miles downriver as it bends
at Beaver and runs west to East Liverpool,
        where my grandfather bought his shoes and worked his first job,
and then turns south for Martin's Ferry, James Wright, and Wheeling.
        I am home today, all of us

standing in front of Kaufmann's windows, waiting
for the light to change, together at last.

A Change of Place

MARY CROW

Shrapnel of morning:
swordlike leaves of the house plant,

forks, knives, scissors.
Light shatters through the window

bags, cans of food, boots,
bits and pieces of makeup.

I am here, not here.
Gray cough of cars rises,

red tiles undulate
green hills undulate:

shimmer of garbage burning.
Counting out the minutes,

I am here, not here.
This year, next year, anytime.

Never. The machine
of my routine is broken.

I want to go home,
put it together again.

Nod

CHRISTOPHER DAVIS

In this mind
beyond dry cornstalks
I come across
my patriarch's abandoned Cadillac

the door gapes
I crawl in
try turning the wheel
it does turn

I tease the radio's knob
twiddling it between pointer and thumb
clicking it on off
clicking it on off

turning it up all the way
hearing nothing
taking in the pain
singing in the pain

Enough. Enough. We interrupt this whining
to broadcast more cowboy yodeling,
the starting of your engines,
gentlemen.

Who'd jump this old thang?
Poisonous pokeweed prods through the bumper.
Why not kiss its dents, fate's public sculpture?
Let it rust out here a few more days.

It might yet get us
where we need to go
if there's no solid place to go
no world called home

Dark Songs: Slave House and Synagogue

LAURENCE LIEBERMAN

— *St. Eustatious, summer 1989*

I.

    A few museum florid paintings by unknown
colorists, but mostly sketches
      in private family albums tell the story —
we children more inclined to trust
      tales we heard of slave days on Granddad's knee
at bedtime than the remote sagas
      we find in our school books today . . . A shipment
of new slaves came, all at once,
      several boatfuls clumped in a caravan:

      serfs in one lead vessel, an echelon or two
above their comrades in chains
      in rear ships, parallel teams of rowers
puffing at the oars to speed
      those sail-masted, multi-sail-driven craft.
The privileged half-freed advance
      troop, whether promoted by bribes, loyalties,
friendship, sexual favors,
      family rank honored across generations,

      or sheer beauty and power of person — those few,
alone, were earmarked for serf
      status: no, not branded or pegged like livestock,
but targeted for low-rank jobs.
      Perhaps no more than four hundred per installment
(from Ghana, Rhodesia), leg-cuffed,
      they were herded like steers — while that vanguard
of cooks, domestics, saddle-
      horsers, disembarking first, arranged floor mats

to sleep the maximum number per human stall
in the deep low-ceilinged bins
        of the two-story slave quarters. Chefs, tailors,
laundresses, who slept in makeshift
        huts or tents in the rearyard, had, at least,
some leg room, *private bodyturn space.*
        In the slavehouse, itself, all girls and ladies
were ensconced upstairs, while men
        and boys were marooned to the ground floor.

2.

                    When both levels
                        grow full to capacity, most slaves
                are sandwiched in boxy
                        tight jamups — vertical by day,
                horizontal
                by night: except for sharp jabs in belly, neck, eyes
                        or tendrest parts (breasts, genitals),
        you often don't know your neighbor's knees, elbows,
        bony appurtenances
                (keen-edged, wiry, if underfed on sea
                voyage, as like as not)
from your holy own;

                    but your howls
                        and smart pains — excruciating, most,
                of whip's lash — define you,
                        no confusing your boneaches,
                muscle spasms,
                nausea, or skin rash rawness with your floormate's
                        scorched hide: when skin and bone's
        so mashed, mine into the others, I into Thou,
        agonies keep self
                intact; tiniest remove between Spirit
                entity and entity saves.
Who we be survives. . . .

Some weak slaves,
afflicted with permanent squared
shoulder, humped back,
limbs flattened and malformed,
were disabled
by the crunch of bodies; no few lads suffocated
between more muscular hall mates,
none to blame. At intervals, when slavehouse
quotas ran amok,
open market ships, from South America
and other more distant ports,
arrived: bids for slaves

at townsquare
auction commenced by first light; each
half dozen, or thereabouts,
placed on front doorstoop auction
block, in cluster;
some bidders coerced by shrewd auctioneer to purchase
a mixed gaggle of males, females,
young and old, as one indivisible unit — to speed up
haggling over prices,
finicky tooth checks, sight & hearing tests
as if man needed model-perfect
molars, 20/20 sight,

just to chop
and husk cane all day in the fields;
or lass glamour-shaped hips
and breasts just to scoop proper
bounteous handfuls
of cotton. Each flock might boast a matchless beauty,
or prize strongarm — most slaves sold
for export to distant shores, Statia being chief
transshipment center

for humans, and nonhuman goods, alike,
throughout the Antilles chain
of isles. . . . Before selloffs

in human meat
markets, a normal day in the yards
finds cooks, like modern
caterers, stacking huge supplies
of fast-food grub,
laundresses hauling wagons and carts with mountains
of soiled sackcloth pullovers, baggy
shapeless blouse and shorts, all alike in style,
dull yellowish grey,
loose crosshatched weave of material;
a few sizes are to be stretched
to cover widest spectrum

of body shapes,
women and men in identical garb,
little telling them apart. . . .
I peer into the two-story deep
structure, thin bricks
marvelously even-mortared, still intact today
but for the very few crumbled
or missing slim yellow units; those narrow
interior hallways
resemble storage bins or blank vats
in grain elevators, hardly
fit stable for livestock,

much less brain-
bearing-mammal biped repository;
so few narrow windows, shrunk
to prevent runaways, perhaps,
are raised too high

to collect inflow of trade winds, no East-West matchup
for air streams or ripples of cross-
ventilation: if the inmates weren't asphyxiated
by closest body
cramping, that crush of backs and hips,
they might choke on stale fetors,
so noxious was the stench. . . .

3.

Josser Daniel, my tutor, points across the road,
shoreside, directly opposite
Ye Old Slave House: yet another shipman's stock
quarters fallen into disuse,
idle for one hundred years or more, boarded-up.
This was "de Guvment Guardhouse
and Constabulary joined" (court, too, I suppose,
all functions of arrest, trial,
& jail terms centralized for speedy work shifts) . . .

When British Rear Admiral Rodney laid siege
to Statia, he plundered the gold-
and-silver vaults. Statia, dubbed *Golden Rock*,
had been the wealth jugular —
sea trade megalopolis of the whole Eastern
Caribbean — for decades.
Like today's duty-free Colonies, espoused
for their money laundering
schemes via offshore banks, Statia was haven

for tax evaders at home, drawn to price steals
on ritziest goods the Continent
shipped abroad, at bargain basement markoffs.
Quick as Rodney shut down the Port
with his naval blockade, he set about to fleece

all wealthy merchants — then tried
    to win sympathizers among the local poorfolks.
But a few outspoken mavericks
    painted him History's worst *blackguard, pirate,*

    barbarian, quoting wild Biblical parallels
in both Old and New Testaments
    (so oral historians tell), packed to deliver
the most stinging word portraits
    of his "atrocities" you can imagine, the sole
weapon any might wield against him.
    Sir Rod held all the guns. But ah, what threats
they mustered! The few unnamed —
    though prestigious — writers in their midst

    would spread poison about him to a World Press
(such Global media exchange as
    was viable 200 years back): they'd brand him
close kin to Attila the Hun!
    Since his most acid and eloquent accuser
was a prominent Jew, Rod staged
    a surprise police raid on a Friday night
Shabbas Service — in full swing
    in the Upper Town Oranjusted synagogue.

    Ha! Sham holy service, a covert political
town meeting, in disguise, Jews
    plotting sabotage against occupation forces,
so Rodney would bluster and plead
    in his own defense, years later in High Court,
when he answered to charges sworn
    upon him into the docket by Queen's Councilor:
ACTS OF MASS ANTI-SEMITISM
    AND RELIGIOUS CALUMNY disgracing the Crown.

4.

Rodney's armed guards,
undetected, surround the old Synagogue
where all but a smidgin of some three-hundred-odd
adult Statian Jews
are congregated, arrest them en masse
(not a soul among them can slip
through Rodney's net), and swiftly transport the lot
to this Guardhouse, three ships at the ready, armed to gunnels'
galley teeth, all sails furled to deport them —
the whole Congregation:
chainlocked indoors, thrashing and howling, for fear
they be pilloried, throttled, lynched, or rent
by firing squads

at daybreak. . . . Before dawn,
they're whisked to the pier, ropetied in threes
or foursomes, mouths gagged, heads bag-covered
to cloak their faces
from stray passersby (though all citizens
are warned by Curfew Broadsides
to stay indoors or risk police detainment,
not to say sniper fire); those who resist, the hysterics,
flinging themselves sideways or backward on the wharf,
are dragged aboard
by their heels, heads clumping like loose potatoes
in the sacks; those upright, the stoics,
are stampeded

from dock to shipdeck —
the whole forced exodus carried off, lickety
split, in ten minutes flat. . . . Thus, the near bulk
of Island Jewry,
third and fourth generation Dutch families
who hail back to the civic

roots of Colonial days, are Shanghaied, lugged
to twelve-miles-distant St. Kitts, abandoned on woodsy
shoreline: huge death bounties sworn on their heads,
if their postered mugs
be spotted in Statia. . . . Sir Rodney's return home,
months hence, greeted by scathing headlines
in London Press:

ATTACKS ON DUTCH JEWS
DEPLORED BY HOLLAND, Admiral Rodney's conduct
in Statia viewed as "heinous, verging on Holy War,
and UN-BE-COM-ING
to any agent of Her Majesty the Queen
on the High Seas," these charges
upon Rodney's honor carrying far more sting
than vandalism, pillaging, or no-holds-barred piracy
(the latter, just the spoils of war by a turn
of the tongue); no record's
extant that Rodney had slain even one Jew —
but his impulse to wipe the whole Isle's
Jew-smudged slate

clean, at a single stroke,
smacks of the Third Reich's mass roundups. Secret
abduction of Jews in trucks, railway boxcars, army
transports to the camps;
their sly, devious ruses to keep pervasive
body-snatching under wraps
for those many months. . . . Why, despite Rod's
early departure, did so few Jewish deportees ever return
to Statia? Perhaps the small nation's strand
bore his taint in offshore
mists, a noxious fume of ill spirit hung
suspended in the ghostly sea air. . . .
Today, I explore

                    the awesome blank ruins
         of Synagogue where the worshipers were entrapped,
               a grand void since their going, perhaps never once
                    immersed in formal prayer
               after that day; these walls may never again
have been graced with Cantor's
                    voice waves, or pupil's mime-whispered breath
               chants of Old Testament prayer, some murmured orthodoxy
         of those displaced Jerusalemites smitten
               from this sad haven
                    ever afterwards. . . . And do I hear, again, the song
               of davening, Cantor's sweet lullaby
                    of trilled scripture,

                    the youngest children,
         students of Hebrew reading from the back
               of the holy book toward the front, their fingers
                    groping as they trace
               those richly rounded letters of Hebrew script
alphabets from right to left
                    while they repeat, soundlessly, with their lips
               the Cantor's operatic blessings. . . . *Driven, blindfolded*
         and gagged, bag-shroud-faceless from homeland,
               a family of spirits,
                    dug up by their roots, torn from the soil & hurled
               across the sea, from one tiny Carib
                    outpost to the next.

July 4th

GAYLORD BREWER

It doesn't attack
as scripture details,
with a hammer
and a kiss.
It is not the cankered
worm, the scythe rusted,
the silks
of the dancer or
the bag of coins
discovered in sand.

Instead it is dull,
it prefers the back door,
the porch,
the calico curtains.
It is the bluebird
on the wire, the smiling
snake in the crib,
the last hand of pinochle.
It is a slice
of watermelon.
It is the face behind
the mortgage desk,
the blank face
carrying the ball, a man
staring at a sprinkler
in disbelief.
It is the moon rocket
and Roman candle.
It is the polished auto.
It is the newspaper.

It is every sticky plate
licked clean
by a mongrel dog.
It is a beer bottle
and a new blouse.
It is membership
in the club
of the cross,
a shovel
forgotten in the garden,
a shopping cart,
the crisp salute
and framed
flag of achievement.
It is the barbecue
of diplomacy
and its white cloth
napkins.

Resist this
at all cost.

Become a moving
target,
a musket
charged with defiance.
Reject their shame.
Weep for the oceans
only, adore the burning
wood,
pray to the blood
of the sacrificed field.
Systematically
eliminate every rumor
you were taught.
Forget each

insidious whisper.
Forget the law.
Listen only
to the tongues
of boots.
Live in cathedrals,
they are everywhere
and empty.

Resist these others
regardless of consequence.

Don't commemorate
them, don't
vote for them.
Don't have cocktails
to honor
their stale jokes
and staler agreements.
They are vipers.
Your friends are not
friends.
Your real family
you have hardly dared
to imagine,
but you can seek them out.
Live not in spite,
but oblivious
of these others.
Your triumph
is sufficient
to assure their defeat.
You needn't think
of them again nor
adorn your

compromise in the
wardrobe of derision.

Live your life
or assuredly
it will
be taken from you,
not by chains
but by necklaces
and serving knives.
Pledge allegiance only
to the song
you've helped
to strangle,
the song of the spirit's
recompense.
Walk straight
into the laughing sun.

Go on, this moment.
Believe it. Freedom
requires only
the faintest courage.
Leap for destruction
like a toad.
Do it blissfully.
A whole sweet language
of ruin
awaits
and not one of them
can speak it.
But you can.
You can flourish
like a rare thing.
You can begin today
to be magnificent.

Internal Exile

RACHEL LODEN

What you will not grieve
is forced on you
in the mirror,
drags like an oar
in black water.

The scented boat
drifts empty
through the stars.
Why must you lie down
where there are no flowers?

What you will not live
eats through the closet
like a moth,
is fattened
on a meal of dust.

You have gone
to that distant city
as some enter a shrine,
not to worship
but to be forgotten.

Bodwin's Madmen

JOHN LUNDBERG

Rain slams the window, ripples the hills,
the wood fence, the empty clothesline
outside this night's Bed and Breakfast

in a town which freed its madmen
two centuries ago; the asylum's funds
dried up and hundreds walked the streets.

Water that fell miles stops an inch
from my face, pressed against the pane.
I see my madman, a black spot climbing

the storm-stirred browns and greens.
He jumped at the thunder's first gray blast,
grabbed the branch he keeps beside our bed

and ran up the dirt and rocks of sheep paths
to the boulders on the highest peak,
where he stands now, tall as a caesar,

leaning against the ripping wind,
he shakes his branch to march the ranks
of clouds rolling under him.

Wide-eyed, electric-veined,
barking for the bolts that light the ground,
he leaps from rock to rock.

With nothing but his hills, his staff,
his fiery mind, he warms the cold
that pelts his face, and looses omnipotent yells.

Autobiography

STUART DYBEK

1

Beneath the dripping udders
of tarpaper roofs
a boy with a stolen jack-knife
pries winter from spring.
That's how I'd begin,
with the smell of mud,
and icicles slipping into rain
as widows pass
unbalanced between shopping bags,
lugging mysterious griefs
by the scruff to novenas.

2

Our Lady of Sorrows,
the Black Virgin of Czestochowa,
was my girlfriend.
Once, while praying,
I saw her smile.
Any old woman
palsied with love and terror
I called *babushka*:
word that transforms
a head scarf
into a grandmother.

3

And every morning was a requiem
or the Feast Day of a martyr —
the priest in black or red,

cortege of traffic, headlights
funneling through incense
under viaducts. While my surplice
settled around me like smoke
my father rode the blue spark
of a streetcar to the foundry
where, in the dark mornings,
the blackened windows glowed
like stained glass.

4

Actually, by noon
the streets were ordinary —
lampposts, sparrows, sewers —
but we knew behind the light
there were other streets
transfigured by a reverence
I can't explain, where
hoodlums stood hooded in violet
like statues in Lent,
and whores were blue
from kissing police.

5

There were autobiographies
at every corner,
legends, litanies, manifestoes,
memoirs in forgotten tongues,
h a silent hiss
in every t'anks.
Autobiographies, but no history,
and by the clang of evening angelus
the babble would condense
into a single, murmured drone

behind a jukebox sax
tailing from an open bar.

6

When it rained on 18th Street
I believed that rain was falling
all over the world. I believed
the neighborhood's war dead were buried
beneath the plaque of their names
on the corner Victory Garden,
and I worried that if people kept dying
the earth would be used up for cemeteries.
I worried that if we kept using
the same notes over
we'd run out of songs.

7

As one grows up, into rebellion,
the dead slowly vanish.
Later, perhaps they reappear.
Sometimes, I'd still catch glimpses
of that parish of phantoms
that childhood borders —
shadows weeping under a crucifix,
spirits expelled from a confessional
wading a gutter under streetlights
as if blood, instead of April muck,
swirled around their black galoshes.

8

I've left out nothing;
these images
are what I knew.
It's not that I didn't listen,

but it wasn't my language
in matters of sex or money.
Whatever else might have been told
was abandoned like excess baggage,
and even now the commonplace
has assumed
the mysterious presence
of the lost.

9

What I finally remember
is feeling free.
That's how I'd end —
walking off down familiar streets
into a republic
where no one is responsible
for the past,
and the common, daily obliteration
is transformed
into a kind of liberty and equality.
Each step a further separation,
my story would recede into a solo
like a saxophone
noodling through broken English.

Confession

STEVE ORLEN

Forgive me, *Adonai*, Lord of the Jews,
God of my ancestors, Almighty *Yahweh*, *Elohim*
Who led Moses out of the wilderness,
But once as a teenager I gave my meek confession
At the Blessed Sacrament Church
So I might not feel so alone.
And now, at night, I cross myself again, yes,
Like any anxious mortal
In the confessional of the kitchen.
I kneel (also forbidden to the Jews)
Before the salt shakers, olive oil, sugar cubes,
I bruise my kneecaps bumping
Across the floor like a *penitente*.
I bow my head with my neck in the noose
As though to stare into my own casket,
And defer like the zebra to the lion, infidel to Allah,
And fold my hands in prayer
To any god who listens late at night,
And ask for absolution.

And thus begins the litany of the imperfect:
Adonai, forgive me, for I have neglected
To sniff the flowers like the lovers do.
I have never stared off into inanimate space
Like the apprentice mystics, for I have little spiritual life
And little intellectual life, for ideas weigh me down
Like heavy jewelry in the earlobes of a rich woman.
Forgive me, *Elohim*, for I've deadened the pain
With whiskey, with leers and laziness,
Pillage of the penis, pillage of the heart, etcetera, etcetera.

I won't tell any more. What good would it do?
At the end, I will stumble, like anyone,
Down Hillside Avenue, that long isthmus between earth and heaven,
With a few neighbors beside me, holding hands.
Some of those flowers I've forgotten to sniff —
A rose for love, a daffodil for humility —
I'll carry before me. I'll walk naked and fat,
With my slippers flapping and my beard grown long.

With every Jew, the good and the bad,
The great and small, with Judah Macabee
And my great-grandmother, Hashe Faige,
About whom many spoke and nobody praised,
With Esther Shapiro, Chaim Haberman, Sore Beyla,
I will lie down and sleep until the Judgment Day,
As it is written.
Will we comfort each other?
About this, the Talmud is silent.

However, here is my only son.
I offer him up, not like Abraham his Isaac,
Nor like Joseph his Jesus, but for consideration only.
He'll walk in my footsteps down Hillside Avenue,
Teetering, with his words spilling from his mouth,
With his sins cupped in one hand, good deeds in the other.
Only then, dear Lord, will you see
What sort of job I have done on this earth.

Ang Tunay Na Lalaki Stalks the Streets of New York

NICK CARBÓ

looking to harvest what makes him happy.
The AA meetings have thrown
him into sacrilegious jousts with Titans

and Gorgons with glowing snake eyes
and leather pants. This is life
without the Filipino bottle,

without the star fruit boogie,
without the *bomba* films. He wears black
Dr. Martens boots because slippers

would expose his *provinciano* feet
to the snow. He wants to ride
the back of a *carabao* and bolt

up Madison Avenue screaming
like Tandang Sora or shout
hala-bira! hala-bira! hala-bira!

like his Isneg cousins in Aklan.
Ay, *susmaryosep!* Such bad behavior
from the "true male" of Filipino

advertising. He looks at his reflection
on a bookstore window, notices
that his hair has grown shoulder-length —

like Tonto in the *Lone Ranger*
he would watch on TV. He turns to the right,
his profile now looks like the young Bruce Lee

as Kato in the *Green Hornet*. Yes,
he realizes it will always be the face
of a supporting character. Rejected

from the Absolut Vodka ads, he decides
to change his name for an upcoming audition
for a Preparation H commercial — *Al Moranas*,

American but with a Filipino flair.

Mask

MARCOS MCPEEK VILLATORO

Today I will consider Tekúm Umán
Whose wooden face hangs on my office wall
For all the passersby to ask "Who's that? Who is he?"

And I can tell the dead Indian's story,
Of how he was the last Mayan to fall
In the flu-ridden skirmishes with the Spanish,

And how he and I hold one thing in common —
My birthday is on his commemoration —
And thus the smile weaves over my humble face

For I have made clear all political positions
By standing behind the wooden mask of a dead man.
When the visitors leave, they do not notice

That I shut the door and dim the lights
And take the wooden sculpture from the nail
And run my finger down the groove of his cheek,

The large bump over his nose, wondering
If the woodcutter thought that necessary
To render satisfied our concepts of a native;

Which as well goes for the multiplumed quetzal
That sits on his only crown, its feathers
Swooping down to cover his ears. The bird has no

Color except brown. Its eyes reflect his own —
Large, open, empty — honest as a mask.
Of course I try it on. I press the curve

Of its backing against my confused face
And dance a fine rain dance, back and forth
Across my white carpet, newly shampooed.

The Reappeared

VIJAY SESHADRI

Long after we stopped remembering, word of him
drifts back from the coast
to let us know he's still hanging on

in someone else's place and time,
living in a shed in their ivy-choked gardens —
his head shaved, his altered face,

the skin in patches under his eyes.
Supposedly though he's still tender and wise;
and having found out it's the same there as here —

the heat breaking out of its sack,
the stars wobbling on their black thrones —
he's made up his mind to never come back.

It's all the same; and on its verge
the borderless ocean scrawls and scrawls
reiterations which repeat

that it's all the same,
and he can fall into it and never change,
resurface, and simply swim away.

In California

KATHY FAGAN

one either believes in God
or believes one is
God. Like the freeway, you can't drive on
both sides at once.
Medians themselves are horticultural
phenomena. And from every direction there is
vista, there is grande.
There are places called
Vista Grande.
I have seen them myself,
have the photos to prove it.
I have stepped from my car in a glockenspiel
shirtfront and conducted
orchestras.
I have held in my hand a baton of sky,
while the hills looped gold
green   silver   black,
and the automatic tollbooths rang and rang,
lifting and letting fall
their braceleted arms.

In California there is more
land than ocean; we will not
discuss then, in this poem, the ocean.
Let us place coins where its eyes used to be
and insist instead,
as wisteria insists —
the insistent part of the wisteria — on
architecture. Consider
the bungalow, the overpass, the balcony
balustrade as muscular as any Mister

Atlas, tiny kites wound
round his triceps. And the palms:
it's not just headdresses with them
but mufflers, full-length
raccoon coats, that trailing
perfume of fennel and sage, a dust
that will not dust
off. Not off the palm, not off the grape,
not off the live oak or
the dead. Rolling the piers and streets and orchards,
only the fog can slick it down.

I take it back
about the kites. I see now the five points,
the pentagons of morning
glory choking the balcony,
and potted nasturtiums on the landing
gleaming. How our grandmothers favored them,
the old flowers, old edible
flowers. Like the old
stories, they have it all:
feet of clay, suits of mail,
coats of brine, hoops of gold. . . .

Red Aster, who made you?
The Sun made me.
And who, Red Aster, ringed you with gold?
You have, Maestro, who planted me here.

East River Prison Barge

HUNT HAWKINS

The powerboats cut the water
like long, white knives. Beefy men,
some too young you'd think to afford
the pop, steer from perches
while even younger women catch
the sun. Past Roosevelt Island,
the townhouses in the fifties
with their leafy trees. They favor
naughty names: Hooky, Delinquent,
Renegade. Near Manhattan Bridge
they pass the barge, gray, five stories,
rolls of razor wire atop chicken mesh
where inmates hang, blots of graph paper,
all black and brown men yelling
what they'd do with the playgirls' holes.
The diesel roar drowns them out.
"No Docking!" says the sign. Shining in the light,
the cruisers round the Battery, head for the Narrows,
escape for their long weekends.

The Sirens of Los Angeles

BRUCE BOND

All summer as the blacktop softens, drugged
in an ether of smog and visible heat,
you can hear the car stereos hard at work,
the bass throb of vans blooming at stoplights,
a shushing window and its flash of song.

Light burns on a fender in a sluggish tide
of fenders, the whole flammable basin
now littered in dry birds and foxtails.
I love this city, however long I soak
in the shadows of my shirt, in the dark

plumes of riot and angry script, a wash
of syringes under the pier. It's the dark
a singer leans her mike to, saying *no*
to the world the way a child says *no*.
Palms beat their shredded wings in the sun.

They too are waiting for the earth to move.
No word for the phone-pole repairman lashed
to his mast, a song blasting in his headset,
drowning the street in solitary music.
An ambulance parts the waters of our traffic —

one life, one life, it says — and the cars
wash back to bury its path. When the sun sets,
it trails a fluorescence of theaters
and taillights, the fresh stupor of children
streaked in purple; there's an art to forgetting

that oceans know, swallowing the day's pill
of fire. The floodlit heads on billboards lay
their layers over the heads before them,
wave on wave of blind eyes and giant teeth.
Every day the world is growing younger.

We could drive to the darkened crest and look back,
the city cracked open like a radio.
In the distance a living wire of sound.
Copters prick the alleys with their spotlights.
We could work our lives with wax in our ears

and fool no one: even in our sleep we hear
the echoes blossom in the throats of dogs —
or is it our own sleeping throats we hear —
each heart a bottle of blood impatient
for land and feasting, longing to be poured.

Beach Rogue

JOANNE LOWERY

Unevenness and sand giving way
make his walk lopsided as if
he has stumbled on a desert island.
Farther than the last human footprint,
to the lighthouse with its smashed tip.
Neither brown rocks nor amber
neither white, black nor pink
climb into his pocket. He's looking
for a gold doubloon to wash up,
Shakespeare's lost sonnet in a bottle,
a map to where the gulls
will run up to him
crying out his eminent name.

Plus Shipping

BOB HICOK

Inspired by Kokopelli, Golfer-Pelli
is a fun-loving symbol for our times.
— advertisement

Certainly it was a premonition of a Navajo warrior that men
in plaid would take up sticks and club a ball into a hole's

submission. And that a god of prosperity and joy, flute
player, source of the wind's conversational obsessions,

secretly longed to represent the beef-fatted, tax-sheltered,
divot-spewing tribe in their hunger for real estate

made green and blemish free, acres of fertilized eternity.
It happened like this: someone named Stan or Rita

spanked their cell-phone open in Manhattan traffic, called
Lou Ellen or Robbie and went on at an ecstatic pitch

about a program they saw on the Learning Channel last night
that documented cave paintings in Arizona of this guy

with hair like spiders and a body twisted as if
he'd swallowed a hurricane, and wouldn't it make a hot

nick-knack if we put him in knickers with a seven-iron
in his hands? And later, after the market research,

after paying one company to come up with a name, another
to design the eyes, hips, the casual-yet-indigenous-gestalt

needed to represent a sport built around the prophecy
of leisure, Stan or Rita will confess to something like

inspiration, a little zing, a small frisson disrupting
their preoccupation with fear that screamed low

cost, high profit. And I wouldn't mind if I were ten
or drunk most of the time, if I'd missed

even half the commercials utilizing the dramatic skills
of Super Bowl quarterbacks, the winks of senators

who reached for president but fell one scandal short,
wouldn't care if I could forget Michael Jackson

trying to sell his crotch, Elizabeth Taylor
hustling the diamonds of her scent, if just once

someone would stand before a camera and simply say
I've made this offensive thing but won't leave you alone

until you send me ten bucks. Golfer-Pelli's destined
for mantles, to fill that hole between vase and clock

where space bleeds, needing the bandage of artifact.
And what of the Buddha alarm clock, Shiva spice rack,

the shoe polisher in which red and green fuzzy wheels
pop from Mohammed's ears and spin your leather clean?

Give it time and you'll get your crack at each
and more, for as we eat and sleep there's someone

flipping through a magazine, strolling the open veins
of ruins, touching forgotten texts, sculpted faces

of a people centuries gone, who can't help but think
there's beauty and sorrow and money in every one of these.

David's Rumor

LIAM RECTOR
— *for Dave Wale*

I am busy doing drawings
    for the upcoming publication
Drawings of Schizophrenics in Closed Institutions.
I am busy doing drawings
    for the upcoming publication
Drawings of Schizophrenics in Closed Institutions
      because angelic voices will sing
      if I draw lost enough to listen

      and because it quiets the doctors down
      since they are anxious
      to see the book published
      and to have my efforts included. . . .

If I could find the right line, I could balance my entire design.

      Not everyone has a career,
      but the doctors have one, each of them,
      and the publication of the book *should* help to secure

      that section of their lives.

Alice, across the hall, is doing
a goodbye drawing. The doctors
are wary of this impulse
on her part, noting that Alice
says goodbye
too often. They encourage her to talk
of her plans, should she be released,
or of her past,
  should she end up staying.

Alice tells them it's a "picnic,
a picnic in a light drizzle."

Here in the hospital Alice,
who killed Frank, crosses the hall each night
into my doorway and says,
"Frank, is that *you*, Frank?"

> In my drawings I omit Alice
> and concentrate
> on calling forth the hall. Schizophrenia,
> in this book, is another way of saying
> *across the hall.*

In the public room, the section where we sit and watch,
some read the newspaper while getting
the national news off the tube.
That way, if you read and listen,
you get the feeling
that the news is really coming at you,
that it might finally amount to something.

Of late I have begun to think,
I get the impression,
that our lives are being moved
by some very public rumor.

We, in darkness, picture ourselves alone
with some sort of headline: *Man Claims He Got Away
with Murder,* that sort of thing. . . .
We read as if dreaming and are then
dreamt as if living. Between
the solitary and the public, the rumor.
We picture ourselves closed-in, whirring,

but I doubt that.

In the drawings I stress
(and then surrender to) the fact
that there is some very "hard news"
in all of us, a murderer
for each of us, and that this is how
all these reports, these *mayhems*,
finally do manage to reach us.

Pavese, the Italian, said that each
murderer is a timid suicide. Alice,
who killed Frank, wanders each night
for all of us, wondering who Frank
really is.

If I could find the right line, I could balance my entire design.

George, who lost his mind after losing
Carol, lives far down the hall. George says
Carol's infidelities at first made him want
to do away with himself, to surrender, but that later,
through the help of the doctors,
he realized it was Carol
that he wanted to kill
all along, that his impotence
was caused by a gun
that he didn't want to point
towards her, a thing he didn't want to see
go off.

None of this surprises me.
The drawings get so lost because the hall
is so wide. You come through a cauldron
before you ever sight home. . . .

My own crime bears no mention.
It was an argument, a debate gone wrong,
an affection historied into the berserk.

My work here now, my *calling*,
is to get these lines down right, to *delineate*
their deep gossip, that precise chamber
where they, right or wrong, do yak sublime. . . .

    And the doctors,
    the doctors say the book will receive
    national distribution and I'm glad,
    yes glad with all my heart,
    for that. Ambition,
    which is finally what we do to each other,
    will undoubtedly see this project
    into its rise and quiet. . . .

And the lines go off, they wander. . . .
If I could find the right line, it could balance, balance
this riot, that hall, that vacancy and pressure
wherein we draw towards goodbye.

Big Thicket Requiem

H. PALMER HALL

— An elegy in six parts for James Byrd, Jr.

I.

Seven miles from the highway, down
    trails truckling through cypress trees —
    the sun a hint of fire edging the leaves —
        a family of beavers builds a home. Never

enough to participate from the bank
    of tooth- and tail-crafted pond, I shed
    shirt and pants, strip to bare truth
        and wade into brown water, mists

still rising in the stippled day. Toes
    squish through ripe mud, bubbles ooze up.
    Sink down, descend days and years,
        into first light. Sunlight, banding in waves,

breaks into thin beams between leaves
    and falling, falling, splatters knees
    and belly, chest, penis, pale buttocks,
        paints the years. Only the sounds

of splashing, rap of a woodpecker on dry bark,
    rustle of armadillos rooting through damp
    leaves, breath heavy, alien. So and, again,
        so. A white heron, immense in beauty,

breaks flight, dips down, beak open, splashes
    white from bank to bank. A water snake seeps
    from a broken limb, no noise, only silence except:
        a steady rain of leaves, the drop of dead limbs.

II.

Blacktop yellow stripe down the middle
    they dragged a living man down
    down until they dragged a dead man
        broken into pieces

on either side, tall pines, planted
    every ten years pulped after growth
    tall enough to mill the paper
        to publish the obituary

these woods have a dead man in them
    broken shredded into black asphalt
    head legs torso scattered like needles
        deep woods whisper here

a thousand people drive over red specks
    spread droplets of raging tears but
    a dead man's dying cannot roll dark
        thicket into shining light

III.

A moment in the clearing:
    surrounded by sound
    the buzz of a yellow fly
        attracted by the repellant

used to keep him away,
    a woodpecker probes the bark
    of a loblolly pine, squirrels
        skitter along dry branches.

No water here, the hard pan
    scrabble beneath a layer
    of brown clay supports
        orchids, sundews, pitcher plants.

A tropical savanna, hot,
    humid, where trapped moisture
    cannot sink far beneath roots
        digging deep in parched meadow.

Plants here find dampness,
    food, where they can, eat flies, gnats,
    small insects, turn their faces
        into the soft breeze, no chewing sound,

only soft, slow dissolution
    the clear liquid of digestive juices.
    A few miles away, cars move
        swiftly down the asphalt road.

Slash pines grow in even rows:
    flattop groves twenty, thirty
    feet high. Nothing lives there
        not designed for the harvest.

IV.

Make a list of the lost:
    Ivory-Billed Woodpeckers,
    the Witness Tree, red wolves,
        turkeys, passenger pigeons. Gone.

Twelve men and women in Jasper
    sit quietly waiting for the start
    of what did not end at the tail
        of a pickup dragging terror

in the dark. Along the highway,
    the bodies of armadillos and skunks,
    beer cans, cigarette stubs, used
        condoms, body parts. Waste.

In this small savanna where plants
    kill their prey, live natural lives,
    do what they have always done,
        sunlight brightens wild orchids.

A single blossom, lovely lavender
    drifts down the creek, dodges a snag,
    washes around a drifting log under a low
        bridge on Huff Creek Road.

v.

Dark currents lurch around a buried
    limb. Listen: some kind of animal
    I've never heard and cannot make out
        lurches through the weave of undergrowth.

I sleep almost, hold my head up as long
    as I can. Bubbles rise from somewhere
    under brown water, turtle water, detergent for
        whatever washes up, drenches through.

Here, when late sun splashes, no bleaching
    agent leaches color from the ground, an inch
    of long leaf pine needles coats the thicket floor,
        rich earth — damp, brown — feeds green and red lichens.

A covey of quail, busy-muttering, bustles along
    a trail, does not see me, their own world of alert
    detects only present danger, sharp movement. They
        vanish through a titi stand, leaves close around them.

vi.

A moment in the thicket, that moment
    when the dark is darkest and briefly
    everything is as silent as anyone could want,
        somewhere above tall trees, canopies

woven tight together, stars so bright they
        could light the world glitter coldly. Only
        a moment, then a rustling from the titi
                stand, small trees ringed with yellow-green

algae, and the sun breaks. Black surrenders
        to gray, leaves grow translucent, glow
        in the early light that has not, will not,
                reach the ground, a small speck in a baygall,

beam piercing through an opening. Nearby
        a mockingbird cries, cardinals sing to each other,
        a jay shrieks through the morning haze. So
                good to be alive at this moment when

the world awakens and a single ray
        of light blinds you to everything even
        this spot where you sit on the cool ground —
                soft, moist, and in the light white wings flutter.

Rural Particles

BARRY SILESKY

Asters, yarrow, an enormous oak at the edge of the bank leading down
to the river. Each leaf, each blade of grass is part of the force a man's trying
to measure as he walks toward the water. And they're strong; they hold him
here with this arrangement of particles: the blue house, a crane, a handful
of blackberries — but they're hard to figure. As soon as he gets an idea, a pipe
starts leaking and the whole equation changes. He thinks there's a way to
understand it so he keeps reading: up, down, strange; hard to believe this is
science. It's something he takes on faith — a voice on the phone, a rocket past
the moon — then a woman walks through the door announcing the African
drought, kids out of the question, and he's up half the night with her. Where's
the chapter that tells what to name this? The formula for its vector?

So he's put the place up for sale. If someone's buying, it could be a chance
to start over, or at least continue with the new luggage these pieces might fit
into. If he keeps shuffling the figures, he thinks the new particles these weak
interactions bring in and out of the problem — the job in the city, the woman,
the moon — might coalesce into the sequence that points the way. He thinks:
I can quit smoking for good, cut off my beard. It's been years since I've been
to the mountains. But when the offer comes, he can't bring himself to take
it. The pages go by so fast the woods blur as the fall's first storm moves out
the summer. Then the wood chips fly as he piles the oak for another winter
he won't be there to see, and it's time to go. It doesn't make sense at all. It's
something he understands.

Symmetry

BARRY BALLARD

This body's stretched with its patchwork tilled so
deep that even friends (who stand back in clouds)
say they witness the betrayal that's plowed
through the tight symmetry, the overflow
of neighboring swamps that causes the saplings
to fold their roots, and each explanation
to drop like yellow withered leaves unstrung
from this choice and poisoned imaginings.

But if I've already raked the dry leaves
into fires and accepted the charred
consequences of what they call "mistakes,"
couldn't I plant a field of blossomed needs
and cultivate my time without them, far
from a need for fences with no escape?

Teshuvah

LAMAR THOMAS

Gathering up all the dolphins
in my dreaming.
I'm coming home.

Hearing the hooves of great Pan
clicking on the stones of Manchester Beach.
Mystery no longer holds me.

Taking down the black veil
from the mirror in my hallway.
I cannot worship death.

The arrow news is swift
and true, and yet, long flies
the heart hiding from itself.

Nomad: I hasten through fields
of poppy and sunflower.
The fragrance weaves into my hair.

The horizon withdraws
and I have no prayers to sunset.
I now follow a narrow human shore.

After the opiates and the lost loves,
how can I become myself?
The key to all this is redemption.

And what is that redemption?
Every thing that leads toward Yes,
toward what must be made romantic
in a world that says No.

Max Beckmann & Quappi in Blue

J. J. BLICKSTEIN

1924 Pleasure
possible bed   fanatic   clean
resigned temple in violent colors
try to remember the ritual
the unused linen shaved from wood
the sacrifice in humanity
when sex is another condition
tight quarters in sequel of order
violence that leaves no stain in the angel or
in the compact measures of civilians at war
to reconcile the stitches
in that vision
seduction by odor and the shape of her breast
she is strong
tobacco and sweet luxury forming her thigh
small rooms and roses contain her well
makes the skin breathe louder
in brown in blue
the flaws and oversized nostrils leave us lovely   we
with my gold crown and enormous crayons
my eyes come larger kinder rounder than her ass
my delight in the shadows where observed
she rests

Interlude 1933 stainless steel skyline in the black backdrop
of the imagination trespassed into a girl with a yellow cat

Exile 1937
The parade in soft glass with waltz and smothered brass
folds meticulous in the armband of the ballroom
and pamphleteer   all these toys and crimes

stolen from the imagination in red and black
uncloak the precision of the premonition
in the burning wheel

exiled degenerate from what is most private in the
mind —
from what was a language of freedom in the human dream
to the smokestacks of our evolution
raped in the real
we must be careful in our thoughts   they become
and we defiled and ineffectual cannot
move in our portraits and oils
as reality conquers our imagination and we become a dream in rooms
left to reinvent our escape

Self Portrait with Horn 1938
Max Beckmann and Quappi in Blue 1941

gold thread kiss the scissors together in the miniature
lifestyle   the exile and hats forever in other rooms
each room a portrait with demonic flowers beneath
the walls   we in suits dressed for dinner in rooms
we will never leave   banished   in the garden

fall back to texture as its own end   the human relationship
no compromise on form
man woman woman together repelled and attracted
by the instruments and decor of our sex
flesh and clothing   so much time to be imagined in the garden
so much time with desire
and the woman with the mandolin between her legs like a swan
on a yellow blanket and red sofa 1950
large warm brunette with perfect tits conquering the distraction
of the night music and bullets of the mother tongue
she welcomes him into her false sleep

he welcomes us to the greater mystery   participation
where the neck of the instrument   alert   gazes
and memorizes lips tongue and the rhythm of breast
before departing with her sound

The last portrait of self   in blue jacket
without hat   speaks perfectly anonymous
and indulges elegant with the exiled self
in the neon light of "American Painting Today"

Goodnight in Brooklyn through the park and stainless steel skyline
back to the bed and walls exhaling forever into
the tattooed crown and the reality
of the undreamed imagination

Green Ash, Red Maple, Black Gum

MICHAEL WATERS

How often the names of trees consoled me,
how I would repeat to myself *green ash*
while the marriage smouldered in the not-talking,
red maple when the less-than-tenderness flashed,
then *black gum, black gum* as I lay next to you
in the not-sleeping, in the not-lovemaking.

Those days I tramped the morass of the preserve,
ancient ash smudging shadows on stagnant pools,
the few wintry souls skulking abandoned wharves.
In my notebook I copied plaques
screwed to bark, sketching the trunks' scission,
a minor Audubon bearing loneliness like a rucksack.

And did the trees assume a deeper silence?
Did their gravity and burl and centuries-old patience
dignify this country, our sorrow?

So as I lay there, the roof bursting with invisible
branches, the darkness doubling in their shade,
the accusations turning truths in the not-loving,
green ash, red maple, black gum, I prayed,
in the never-been-faithful, in the don't-touch-me,
in the can't-bear-it-any-longer,
black gum, black gum, black gum.

Comcomly's Skull

JIM BARNES

Comcomly's skull is coming home.
That wily one-eyed Chinook chief,
whose other bones are scattered from
the grave, keeper of slaves, thief,
will have his fore-flattened skull
and, gods willing, his fevered soul

back, buried finally and forever,
courtesy Ilwaco, Wash., Cemetery
Association. According to Meriweather,
head of the Chinook Council, "We
plan, for the event, a salmon bake;
we'll call it Chief Comcomly Day."

August 12. Slow birds tread the sun
above the open grave. The priest —
Baptist or Episcopalian,
pagan or seventh son of Crow — casts
a shadow too long for the time
of day. His eulogy turns on rhyme.

After salmon and wine, song birds
and a soft coastal rain begin.
The sun has sunk into the clouds.
Somewhere over against a mountain
a lone wolf lets out one wild howl.
The earnest sky begins to fall.

An unexpected hail. Hell
on dogs and birds. The sky can't hold
its wrath or praise long enough for all

this pomp and circumstance to mold
ancestral flesh onto his skull.
The eyes stay empty. The sky grows full.

Looking for Level Green

JUDITH VOLLMER

Seneca once told a whit man
the way to Fort Duquesne was
"West. Two days through forest.
Then cross a long, level green."

Now a suburb of the suburb of
Monroeville, home of the nondestructive
Nuclear Facility. No uranium on site.
No plutonium. No more blue collars.

Ten minutes, though, and you're in a green
pocket called Daugherty's Grove
where my parents fell in love
and where bluebells drift behind gaspumps
standing sentinel to a sad forest of dwarves.

Ten minutes from the fat cool mall & condos
framing the thruway
stands Rountop, old burial mound, ignoring
anyone's wishes to dig bones or potsherds or memories.
A girl can lie down there and not think, for once.

And ten minutes from the weapons site
that has no dripping, leaking
or raw oily places
slouches the Shades of Death
where a woman killed herself for love.
There's nothing but
dark pines down in there
alive and holy, alive with her.

Two Uncertainties

PAUL HOOVER

There is eternity to blush in.
— Djuna Barnes

Around the attic bird, the century is silent;
gathers utter ghosts in scattered dust displays.
Afloat in that window, not even a star approaches like a dog.
Nothing is left to desire: rain in open cars,
gasoline fires. History is ending.

We are not, however, among those voices off.
We are the ones in prose whose form
is finally shapeless, except for these constraints.
With the labor of planets turning,
please bind us to a version of ourselves.

What Hurts

GUSTAVO PÉREZ FIRMAT
— *for Virgil*

We are called broken
because we do not humor the age,
mask our distemper, dress our disdain
in vests and valentines.
We are called broken
because we do not settle,
we roil, we wrack, we wreck
ourselves and our wives and our children,
ourselves and our friends and their children,
ourselves and our wives and their friends.

Truths and troubles we tell them,
hurts and hatreds we tell them,
how it all began and how it will end,
who did what to whom and for what reason,
who's to blame and what the punishment should be.

We spare them nothing.
We tell them *todo*, then go on to more.
We break them with our brokenness
until they are broken too.

Moment

JANE HIRSHFIELD

A person wakes from sleep
and does not know for a time
who she is, who he is.

This happens in a lifetime
once or twice.
It has happened to you, no doubt.

Some, in that moment, panic;
some sigh with pleasure.
How each later envies the other,
who must so love their lives.

Walking Back

WILLIAM TROWBRIDGE

I have no business here, a bearded stranger
circling the block, beginning to draw looks
from the man pruning his forsythia, the housewife
who calls the children in from jump rope.
Dutch elm disease has thinned the landscape,
let afternoon sunlight glare off grass and sidewalks.
Everything looks too new. Our house is green now,
with patio and lawn where tufts of rye grass
used to stall our mower till my father
took to working weekends at the office.
Even our front-yard maple's forgotten
my mark beneath thirty-five new rings.
Up the street, Skrija's grocery store
has lost its musty heart of oak
and penny candy. A neon sign announces
"Guns and Ammo" above barred windows
and a yellow metal door. Still, there's the
bump at Sixtieth and Grove — ready as ever
for the next no-hander showing off for his idea
of the girl who'd like his looks — and the blue jays
and the locusts and the tack of ripe asphalt.

Like those who stare, I wonder what I want,
whether I'm dangerous or simply need directions.
Today, hundreds, maybe thousands of us search
the old neighborhoods for clues: initials in a sidewalk,
a rusty nail pounded in a tree, a wish still floating
near the school, where a small ghost, waiting
on the last bell, rubs the shiny nickel in his pocket.

A Flock of Phantom Limbs Gather at the Border

BRUCE BOND

An amputee is a brood of indecisions;
the scent of smoke lingers in her shirt;

refugees crowd the bare plain passing the secrets
of their diseases, on their backs the iron rainclouds

melding; a child scours a rock with her gaze
as if to eradicate the face she sees there;

they keep coming to this place, faces
uneasy as cities flowing into cities, where linen-tents

flap their bloodless wings, where sleep
endangers, where the silence of the exhausted

is the dropped jaw of a sanctuary wall;
behind them an army of scribes and bits of char

write one history over another; a holy city
is an insomniac book: black page, black page;

a man is entering an alien airspace, a cold front
of bodies moving over the face of the earth;

he carries his language like a bag
of bread and disinfectant; he is not quite

in this nation he's in, but he's close
approaching the great collapse when sky groans

like a long-locked gear and the thunderhead
opens its thick fist; he does not stop walking

where he lies, flecked in sores and the first few drops;
he does not roll into the palm of the state;

he hears the thrum of planes like some immense stone
bearing down through a hole in the world.

Elegy Written on a Blue Cement Gravestone (To You, the Archeologist)

BENJAMIN ALIRE SAÉNZ

What history is:
a mound of gathered rocks. In time the rocks will
melt, will turn to dunes of sand, will blanket everything
you fought your wars to keep. All that work and worry;
the countless sleepless nights; the house you built
and loved (thirty years of paying right on time);
the perfect car that lasted forty years, the ring
you gave your wife, the clothes you bought your sons.
All buried now, those things (the worries, too).
Remember this: everything will die except the desert
sands. Everything will fade except the ashes of the
earth we filtered through a smelter's lonely tower.
The smelter, too, has died. And one day, soon, the tower
will be dust (not unlike your car; not unlike your
house; not unlike your wife). All debris and ashes.

*

Pick up a spade. Roll up your sleeves
and dig. Wipe the sweat from your brow. Then dig deeper,
deeper still. You cannot stop. You're a worker now.
Pray to God to find the heart you lost here long ago.
You need it now. Pray. Dig. Laugh (if you can) at
the blatant irony: to end your days doing what you
hated. Fated to become an archeologist.

*

See this artifact? Laid with crude cement and painted
blue. Deep as moaning from a mourner. Deep as scars
on Jesus' arms and feet. A gravestone, a marker, not

granite, not marble, a common monument befitting
the class and taste of the deceased (or the survivors).
The inexpensive cross with corpus (bought retail
at a shut down shop on Stanton Street). History
is buying and selling. History's an aisle of icons.
History's a birth, it's a funeral. History's a rose
made of plastic. History's a grave with no date.
History is broken cement. History's a litany
of questions: How many minds wasted at the plant?
How many bones fractured? Broken? Mended? How
many hearts shattered like a cheap ceramic cup?
Find the pieces, archeologist! Reconstruct the
hearts! Remember this: these ruins guard their
solitude. They've fought their wars, and fight them
still. Ask anything you like.

> You *will not* make them speak.

*

> A son or son-in-law, in grief,
designed this monument. A daughter picked the paint.
They thought their work would make the world remember.
There was a day: this painted blue cement was God
in heaven's envy. Not now. No longer. That day is
dead. The wind and rain, the ceaseless sun, the endless
days. The work, the dust, the drought. It's broken
now, this stone that praised a life. It's broken now.
The earth will break us all.

Poem from Across the Country

MARGOT SCHILPP

The flowers have checked their suitcases.
In the old mythology, flowers could speak:
Day moves across the meadow;

autumn shadows break our necks.
In the waiting room of the heart
we all sit against the walls and read

dated magazines. Something looks
over the shoulders of the crowd
and beckons: maps end

the curiosity we must have had
about time; crossings plotted
are no adventure.

It is always like this. Suits and skirts
walking themselves to their stations,
another penny spent and rolling

under the wheels' economy.
One by one we are called
and we go, but I can see,

even with the image of hypnotic light
that paralyzes me when my eyes close:
another day is gone.

Is is; Is isn't.
One of these is true.
I thirst; there is no water.

Mind the oases of desire that fling
themselves at your throat, butterflies
committing suicide against your throat.

You won't have come
upon it yet, but it is there.
There must be a way to lose yourself

now, to resist cartography
and physics. How much
can it hurt to swallow

loss? I looked and was burned,
a heliotrope turning to track
the sun across my mind,

wanting it
to heat me so that I didn't
burn from the inside out.

Miami

MONIFA LOVE

— *for David and Evans*

one could give up writing

ask those who keep the odor
of exile on their skin and miles
of dusty earth clogging their throats
ask those who crave west coast chrysanthemums
and canyon homes on a frontier of rocks
ask those who leap into midnight roaring

ask those who keen along tungsten-lit arteries
their black low-slung lace veils drawing combat
their stilletos grinding conch into tears
ask those who give away their obituaries
like preachers their first vanity

ask those who pace in the shadow
of rust-colored, windowless cashew trees
and traffic in the saffron buds of springtime
beneath the highway
ask those who burn newly grown
and smoke the song of the melaleuca

ask those who flash along the lanes
who arch in grief like rainbows
reaching but despairing in their motorcars

ask them
the taste of liberty.

How It Begins — How It Ends

RICHARD BLANCO

somewhere, somehow
wind pares down a mountainside
shaves underneath a cliff's chin
or steals a dune from the desert;
somewhere a parched field
is raped by greedy gusts
or a ripe stone is ground
and powdered into a soul;
somewhere something dead
burns alive into a ghost
of carbon-gray ash
a metamorphosis of the solid
into an almost invisible earth

the clever dust slips in
through a cracked-open window
underneath the front door
comes to rest on a tabletop
across the top edge of a frame
over an array of aging photos
on blocks of consumed books.
such relentless disintegration
gingerly settles out of beams
of morning light, the daily gift
collects in the corners of the room
in my eyes, on my hair, over my skin
I taste, inhale, take it in

Contributors' Notes

RALPH ADAMO, who has lived and worked in New Orleans most of his life, edited *New Orleans Review* at Loyola for most of the 1990s. His published poetry books include *Sadness at the Private University, The End of the World*, and *Hanoi Rose*.

KIM ADDONIZIO is the author of three poetry collections, the most recent of which is *Tell Me*. She also coauthored, with Dorianne Laux, *The Poet's Companion: A Guide to the Pleasures of Writing Poetry* (Norton, 1997). She lives in San Francisco.

SHERMAN ALEXIE is a Spokane/Coeur d'Alene Indian from Wellpinit, Washington. In 1992, he received an NEA Poetry Fellowship. In 1998 and 1999, Alexie won the New York Heavyweight Championship Poetry Bout at the Taos Poetry Circus. His several books of poetry include *Old Shirts & New Skins, First Indian on the Moon*, and *The Summer of Black Widows*.

AGHA SHAHID ALI, a Kashmiri-American, calls himself a multiple-exile. Formerly the director of the M.F.A. program in creative writing at the University of Massachusetts–Amherst, he is a poet (his collections include *The Half-Inch Himalayas, A Walk Through the Yellow Pages*, and *A Nostalgist's Map of America*), translator (*The Rebel's Silhouette: Selected Poems by Faiz Ahmed Faiz*), and critic (*T. S. Eliot as Editor*). Currently he teaches at the University of Utah.

FRANCISCO ARAGÓN, a native of San Francisco and former editor of the *Berkeley Poetry Review*, lived in Spain from 1987 to 1998. He holds a B.A. and an M.A. in Spanish from the University of California–Berkeley and New York University, respectively, and his poems and translations have appeared in *Chelsea, LUNA, Nimrod*, and *ZYZZYVA*, among others.

WILLIAM BAER is the author of *The Unfortunates*, which received the 1997 T. S. Eliot Award. He is also the editor of *Conversations with Derek Walcott*. His work has appeared in *Poetry, Ploughshares, Kenyon Review, Hudson Review*, and other literary journals.

DAVID BAKER is the author of seven books, most recently *Heresy and the Ideal: On Contemporary Poetry* and *The Truth about Small Towns*. He has won awards and fellowships from the National Endowment for the Arts, Society of Midland Authors, Poetry Society of America, and elsewhere. Baker is professor of English at Denison University and poetry editor of the *Kenyon Review*.

ANGELA BALL teaches in the Center for Writers at the University of Southern Mississippi. Her latest collection of poetry is *The Museum of the Revolution*.

BARRY BALLARD's poetry is a reflection of both his formal education (which included studies in theology and philosophy at Texas Christian University) and the sometimes brutal reality of supervising a shelter home for neglected and abused children. He has been published in a number of quality literary journals.

JIM BARNES was born in Summerfield, Oklahoma, and is of Choctaw-Welsh descent. He earned an M.A. and Ph.D. at the University of Arkansas, and was awarded an NEA Fellowship in 1978, a Rockefeller Foundation Bellagio Residency Fellowship in 1990, and a Fulbright Fellowship in 1994. He is currently writer-in-residence and professor of comparative literature at Truman State University, where he also edits the *Chariton Review*.

WENDY BISHOP teaches rhetoric and composition and creative writing at Florida State University. She has published poems and stories in *American Poetry Review*, *Yale Review*, *Western Humanities Review*, and *Cream City Review*, and is the author of *Thirteen Ways of Looking For a Poem: A Guide to Writing Poetry*.

RICHARD BLANCO was made in Cuba, assembled in Spain, and imported to the United States — meaning his mother, seven months pregnant, and the rest of the family traveled as exiles from Cienfuegos, Cuba, to Madrid, where he was born. The family then moved to New York City, then eventually to Miami, where he was raised and educated. He is author of *City of a Hundred Fires*, winner of the 1997 University of Pittsburgh Agnes Starrett Poetry Prize.

J. J. BLICKSTEIN is of Afro-Hebraic descent, a poet/visual artist and editor/publisher of *Hunger Magazine* and Press. He has lived and traveled extensively in Europe and the U.S. Currently, he lives in upstate New York with his wife, a biologist/herbalist.

BRUCE BOND's books of poetry include *Independence Days* (R. Gross Award), *The Anteroom of Paradise* (Colladay Award), and most recently *Radiography* (Natalie Ornish Award). He is director of creative writing at the University of North Texas and poetry editor for the *American Literary Review*.

LAURE-ANNE BOSSELAAR emigrated to the United States from Belgium in 1986. Her poetry collection *The Hour between Dog and Wolf* was published in 1997. Among other publications, her work has appeared in *Ploughshares*, the *Washington Post*, *Marlboro Review*, and *Harvard Review*. She is the editor of

Outsiders: Poems about Rebels, Exiles, and Renegades and of *Urban Nature: Poems about Wildlife in the Cities.*

JOHN BRADLEY is the editor of the anthologies *Atomic Ghost: Poets Respond to the Nuclear Age* and *Learning to Glow: A Nuclear Reader.* His poetry and prose poems have appeared in *Caliban, Ironwood, Key Satch(el), Poetry East, Prose Poem: An International Journal,* and other journals. His book *Love-in-Idleness: The Poetry of Roberto Zingarello* won the Washington Prize, and he was the recipient of a National Endowment of the Arts Fellowship. He teaches writing at Northern Illinois University and lives in DeKalb with his wife, Jana.

SEAN BRENDAN-BROWN currently works as a photographer for the Insurance Commissioner's Investigation Division in Washington. He received an M.F.A. from the Iowa Writers' Workshop and was awarded an NEA grant in 1997. His poems have appeared in *Notre Dame Review, Clackamas Literary Review,* and *Green Mountains Review,* among other literary journals. He has two chapbooks, *No Stopping Anytime* and *Monarch of Hatred.*

GAYLORD BREWER is an associate professor at Middle Tennessee State University, where he founded and edits *Poems & Plays.* His publications include *David Mamet and Film, Charles Bukowski,* and two collections of poems: *Presently a Beast* and *Devilfish.*

MICHAEL BUGEJA, former honorary chair of the National Federation of State Poetry Societies, is on the advisory board of *Writer's Digest* and is special assistant to the president at Ohio University, where he also teaches writing and ethics. His poems have appeared in *Harper's, Poetry, Georgia Review, Kenyon Review, New England Review, Sewanee Review,* and many others. His latest collections are *Millennium's End* and *Talk.*

BRIGITTE BYRD is a French woman who emigrated to the United States ten years ago. She lives in Tallahassee, Florida, where she pursues her doctoral studies in the creative writing program at Florida State University.

RICK CAMPBELL, director of Anhinga Press and the Anhinga Prize for Poetry, teaches English at Florida A&M University in Tallahassee. He has published in many journals, including *Georgia Review, Missouri Review, Prairie Schooner,* and *Tar River Poetry Review.* He has published two chapbooks — *Driving to Wyoming* and *The Breathers at St. Marks* — and has won an NEA Fellowship in Poetry and two poetry fellowships from the Florida Arts Council.

NICK CARBÓ's latest book is *Secret Asian Man.* He has received grants from the National Endowment for the Arts and the New York Foundation for the Arts.

SANDRA CASTILLO was born in Havana, Cuba, where she spent the first eight years of her life. Her poetry has appeared in various anthologies, including *North of Wakulla: An Anthology of Florida Poets, Paper Dance: An Anthology of Latino Poets, A Century of Cuban Writers in Florida,* and *Cool Salsa: On Growing Up Latino in the U.S.* An associate professor senior, she teaches at Miami Dade Community College in Miami, Florida.

G. S. SHARAT CHANDRA, one of India's foremost poets, has lived in the U.S. for many years. His poems and translations have appeared in numerous national and regional magazines, including *Manoa, Many Mountains Moving,* and the *Paris Review.*

MAXINE CHERNOFF is the author of five books of poetry and five books of fiction. She is professor of creative writing at San Francisco State University and editor, with Paul Hoover, of the journal *New American Writing.* She has read from her work in Australia, Belgium, Germany, England, and Scotland.

PETER COOLEY is currently professor of English at Tulane University in New Orleans. He has published six books of poetry: *The Company of Strangers, The Room Where the Summer Ends, Nightseasons, The Van Gogh Notebook, The Astonished Hours,* and *Sacred Conversations.* Since 1970, he has been the poetry editor for *North American Review.*

STEPHEN COREY has published seven collections of poems, most recently *Mortal Fathers and Daughters* and *All These Lands You Call One Country.* His poems, essays, and reviews have appeared in many periodicals, among them *Poetry, Kenyon Review, Shenandoah,* and *Poets & Writers.* His work has been reprinted in various anthologies, including *Passionate Hearts: The Poetry of Sexual Love, Words and Quilts, Writing It Down for James: Writers on Life and Craft, The Random House Treasury of Light Verse* (1995), and *The Pushcart Prize IX.*

MARY CROW, the poet laureate of Colorado, is the author of four books of poetry and three books of translation. She has won a number of prizes, including a Poetry Fellowship from the NEA, a Creative Writing Award from the Fulbright Commission, a Colorado Book Award, and a Translation Award from the Translation Center of Columbia University. She teaches creative writing at Colorado State University.

VICTOR HERNÁNDEZ CRUZ was born in Aguas Buenas, Puerto Rico. Writing poetry since an early age, he has published in *Evergreen Review, Umbra, New York Times Magazine,* and many other publications. Among his books are *Snaps, By*

Lingual Wholes, Red Beans, and *Panoramas.* He lives in Puerto Rico as well as various points on the globe, writing poetry in both Spanish and English.

ROBERT DANA'S most recent books of poetry are *Summer* and *Hello, Stranger.* He edited *A Community of Writers: Paul Engle and the Iowa Writers' Workshop.* He has served as distinguished visiting writer at universities in the U.S. and abroad; after forty years of teaching at Cornell College, he retired in 1994 as professor of English and poet-in-residence.

C. V. DAVIS is a North Carolina native and has earned degrees in English from High Point (North Carolina) University and Florida State University in Tallahassee. In 1999–2000, Davis was a Kingsbury Fellow in creative writing at Florida State University.

CHRISTOPHER DAVIS was born in 1960 in Whittier, California, and is currently associate professor of creative writing at the University of North Carolina–Charlotte. His first collection of poetry, *The Tyrant of the Past and the Slave of the Future,* won the 1988 Associated Writing Programs award, and *The Patriot* won the 1998 University of Georgia Press Contemporary Poetry Series competition. His poems have appeared in many journals, including *Harvard Review, Denver Quarterly, Boston Book Review,* and *Massachusetts Review.*

MICHAEL DENNISON received his Ph.D. in comparative literature from Louisiana State University. He has published poems in many journals and reviews. He is the author of a chapbook titled *Blessing the Bride.* Currently he teaches writing at Carlow College and lives with his wife in Pittsburgh.

TOI DERRICOTTE has published four poetry collections: *The Empress of the Death House, Natural Birth, Captivity,* and *Invisible Dreams: Poems of Embodiment,* as well as a literary memoir, *The Black Notebooks.* She has won numerous awards including two fellowships in poetry from the National Endowment for the Arts, the Pioneering in the Arts Award from National Black Artists Inc., and a Pushcart Prize.

ANA DOINA was born in Romania. After graduating with an M.A. in philosophy and history from the University of Bucharest, she taught high school and adult education. Because of increasing political pressures and social restrictions, she left Romania in 1983. She is now an American citizen and lives in New Jersey with her family. In Romania, some of her poems were published in the national literary magazines: *Romania Literara, Muguri,* and *Sapatmina.*

SEAN THOMAS DOUGHERTY was born in New York City to a mother of Jewish/Okie descent and was raised by an African-American step-dad. A former high school dropout, he has worked in factories, a newspaper plant, and a sawmill. A widely hailed performance poet, he is the author of four full-length books: *The Body's Precarious Balance*, *Love Song of the Young Couple*, *The Dumb Job*, and *The Mercy of Sleep*. He teaches at Syracuse University, where he is completing a Ph.D. in cultural rhetoric.

DENISE DUHAMEL is the author of ten books and chapbooks of poetry, the most recent of which is *The Star-Spangled Banner* (winner of the Crab Orchard Award in Poetry). Her other titles include *Kinky*, *Girl Soldier*, and *How the Sky Fell*. She has read her poems on NPR's "All Things Considered" and appeared on Bill Moyer's PBS special *Fooling with Words*. Her work has been anthologized widely, including three editions of *The Best American Poetry*.

STUART DYBEK was recently a visiting writer at the University of Iowa Writers' Workshop. His poetry, fiction, and essays have appeared or are forthcoming in *Doubletake*, *Five Points*, *Harper's*, and *TriQuarterly*.

MARTÍN ESPADA, a Puerto Rican born in Brooklyn, has won two fellowships from the National Endowment for the Arts, a Massachusetts Artists' Fellowship, the PEN/Revson Fellowship, and the Patterson Poetry Prize. In addition to writing poetry and teaching at the University of Massachusetts, Espada has been a tenant lawyer, a factory worker, and a desk clerk on the night shift at a transient hotel. He regularly volunteers his time to work with disadvantaged city children. His new poetry collection is *A Mayan Astronomer in Hell's Kitchen*.

KATHY FAGAN, author of the National Poetry Series selection *The Raft*, currently teaches in the M.F.A. program at Ohio State University, where she coedits the *Journal*. Her work has appeared in *Antioch Review*, *Denver Quarterly*, *Kenyon Review*, and *New Republic*, among others. She has received the Pushcart Prize for Poetry, Ohio Arts Council Individual Artist Fellowship in Poetry, and Editors' Prize for Poetry in *Missouri Review*. Her latest poetry collection, *Moving & St rage*, won the 1999 Vassar Miller Prize in Poetry.

STEVE FAY's collection of poems, *What Nature* was a finalist for the annual poetry book award given by the Society of Midland Authors, and it has been listed as recommended reading by *Orion*, a premier venue for environmental writing. Fay divides his time between South Beloit, Illinois, and a small acreage in downstate Fulton County. He teaches at Beloit College.

GUSTAVO PÉREZ FIRMAT, a native of Cuba, is the author of several books of poetry. He holds the David Feinson Chair of Humanities at Columbia University.

REGINALD GIBBONS's most recent books of poems are *Sparrow: New and Selected Poems*, which won the 1998 Balcones Poetry Prize, and *Homage to Longshot O'Leary*. From 1981 to 1997 he was the editor of TriQuarterly at Northwestern University, where he is currently a professor of English.

MARIA MAZZIOTTI GILLAN is the founder and director of the Poetry Center at Passaic County Community College, editor of *The Paterson Literary Review* and coeditor of the acclaimed anthologies *Unsettling America: An Anthology of Contemporary Multicultural Poetry* and *Identity Lessons: Contemporary Writing about Learning to Be American*.

PATRICIA GOEDICKE has published twelve books of poetry, the most recent of which is *As Earth Begins to End*. Others include *Invisible Horses*, *The Tongues We Speak*, *Paul Bunyan's Bearskin*, and *The Wind of Our Going*. She grew up in New Hampshire, and lived in Ohio and Mexico before returning to the U.S., first to teach at Sarah Lawrence College and since then at the University of Montana in Missoula.

ALBERT GOLDBARTH has been publishing notable books of poetry for over a quarter of a century, including *Heaven and Earth* (winner of the National Book Critics Circle Award) and his most recent collection, *Troubled Lovers in History*. He is also the author of three volumes of essays. He lives in Wichita, Kansas.

RAY GONZALEZ is the author of five books of poetry, including *The Heat of Arrivals*, and a book of essays, *Memory Fever: A Journey beyond El Paso del Norte*. The editor of numerous anthologies, he received a 1993 Before Columbus Foundation American Book Award for Excellence in Editing. His most recent book of poetry is *Cabato Sentora*. He is professor of English at the University of Minnesota.

DEBORA GREGER is the author of six books of poetry, including *Movable Islands*, *And*, *The 1002nd Night*, *Off-Season at the Edge of the World*, and *God*. She grew up in Richland, Washington, downwind from the Hanford atomic plant. She teaches in the creative writing program at the University of Florida.

LILACE MELLIN GUIGNARD received an M.F.A. from the University of California at Irvine, after which she returned to the southern Appalachians to kayak, write, and teach English and environmental seminars at an experiential high school. Her poems have appeared in *Sundog: The Southeast Review*, *Faultline*, *The Asheville Poetry Review*, *Amaranth*, and others. She is currently studying literature and environment at the University of Nevada at Reno.

H. PALMER HALL grew up in Southeast Texas. Between a two-year period of high school teaching and a brief attempt to register for graduate school, he was drafted and sent to Vietnam as an interpreter/translator for the U.S. Army. His first two poetry collections, *A Measured Response* and *From the Periphery: Poems and Essays*, deal with that war, while his most recent, *Deep Thicket and Still Waters*, is postwar.

BARBARA HAMBY's first collection, *Delirium*, won the Vassar Miller Prize, the Kate Tufts Discovery Award, and the Poetry Society of America's Norma Farber First Book Award. She is also the recipient of a fellowship from the NEA and three fellowships from the Florida Arts Council. Her most recent book, *The Alphabet of Desire*, won the 1999 New York University Press Prize for Poetry. Her poetry has appeared in *Paris Review*, *Iowa Review*, *Kenyon Review*, and *Southern Review*. She lives in Tallahassee, Florida.

LOLA HASKINS has published six books of poems, most recently, *Extranjera* and *Desire Lines: New and Selected Poems*.

HUNT HAWKINS is professor of English at Florida State University. His poetry has been published in *Georgia Review*, *Southern Review*, *Minnesota Review*, *Poetry*, *TriQuarterly*, and many other journals. His book *The Domestic Life* won the Agnes Lynch Starrett Prize in 1992.

BOB HICOK's *Plus Shipping* came out in 1998. *The Legend of Light* won the 1995 Felix Pollak Prize and was an ALA Notable Book of the Year. An NEA Fellow for 1999, his poetry has appeared in *Best American Poetry* and *Pushcart Prize 2000*. He owns an automotive die design business.

BRENDA HILLMAN teaches poetry writing at St. Mary's College in California. Her books include *Death Tractates* and *Bright Existence*, both from Wesleyan University Press. She has received two Pushcart Prizes, a Guggenheim Foundation Fellowship, and the Delmore Schwartz Memorial Award for Poetry. She currently lives in Kensington, California, with her husband, poet Robert Hass.

JANE HIRSHFIELD is the author of four books of poetry, most recently *The Lives of the Heart*, and a collection of essays, *Nine Gates: Entering the Mind of Poetry*. She also edited and cotranslated two collections of poetry by women from the past, *Women in Praise of the Sacred* and *The Ink Dark Moon: Love Poems by Komachi and Shikibu, Women of the Ancient Court of Japan*. Her work appears in *Best American Poetry 1999*, *Atlantic Monthly*, *The New Yorker*, *American Poetry Review*, and elsewhere.

PAUL HOOVER is the author of seven poetry collections, including *Totem and Shadow: New & Selected Poems, Viridian, The Novel: A Poem,* and *Idea,* which won the Carl Sandburg Award. His poetry has appeared in *American Poetry Review, New Republic, Paris Review, TriQuarterly,* and *Partisan Review,* among others. He is editor of *Postmodern American Poetry* and, with Maxine Chernoff, he also edits the literary magazine *New American Writing.*

CAROLINA HOSPITAL is a Cuban-American whose fiction, essays, and poems have appeared in numerous national publications, including the *Washington Post, Prairie Schooner,* and the *Miami Herald,* and her work has been published in more than a dozen anthologies. She has published four books, including *A Century of Cuban Writers in Florida.* She lives in Miami where she teaches at Miami-Dade Community College.

AUSTIN HUMMELL was born in Mandarin, Florida, in 1963. His first book, *The Fugitive Kind,* won the Contemporary Poetry Series Award. His poems appear in the anthology *American Poetry: The Next Generation.* He holds a Ph.D. from the University of Missouri–Columbia and is an assistant professor of English at the University of North Texas.

MARK JARMAN's latest collection of poetry, *Questions for Ecclesiastes,* won the Lenore Marshall Poetry Prize for 1998 and was a finalist for the 1997 National Book Critics Circle Award. He is coeditor of *Rebel Angels: 25 Poets of the New Formalism* and coauthor of *The Reaper Essays.* He teaches at Vanderbilt University.

LARRY WAYNE JOHNS is currently a Kingsbury Fellow in the Ph.D. program at Florida State University. He received a Reader's Choice Award from *Prairie Schooner,* and the first annual Frank O'Hara Award for his chapbook *An Invisible Veil between Us.*

HALVARD JOHNSON was born in Newburgh, New York, and educated at Ohio Wesleyan University and the University of Chicago. He has four published collections of poetry, and his poems have appeared in recent issues of *Puerto del Sol, Gulf Stream, Gargoyle, Florida Review,* and *Confrontation.* He currently resides in Baltimore with his wife, the fiction writer and painter, Lynda Schor.

PETER JOHNSON is founder and editor of *Prose Poem: An International Journal.* He has published two books of prose poems: *Pretty Happy!* and *Love Poems for the Millennium.* His chapbook *I'm a Man* won Raincrow Press's 1997 Chapbook Fiction Contest. He received a creative writing fellowship in 1999 from the NEA.

ALLISON JOSEPH was born in London to Caribbean parents and grew up in Toronto, Canada, and the Bronx, New York. She was educated at Kenyon

College and Indiana University. Currently, she teaches at Southern Illinois University. Her books of poems are *What Keeps Us Here, Soul Train*, and *In Every Seam*.

KASEY JUEDS taught ESL and middle school English before returning to school in 1998; she's currently in the M.F.A. program at Sarah Lawrence College.

GEORGE KALAMARAS is the recipient of a 1993 NEA Fellowship for poetry. His poems have appeared in many places, including *The Best American Poetry 1997, Boulevard, Epoch, Iowa Review, Massachusetts Review, TriQuarterly*, and others. His two chapbooks are *Heart Without End* and *Beneath the Breath*. His collection of poems, *The Theory and Function of Mangoes*, won the Four Way Books Intro Series in Poetry Award.

RODGER KAMENETZ is the author of *The Missing Jew: New and Selected Poems, Stuck: Poems Midlife*, as well as *Terra Infirma, Stalking Elijah*, and *The Jew in the Lotus*. In 1995 he created the first Louisiana Diaspora People's Conference at Louisiana State University, where he teaches poetry and nonfiction writing and directs the Jewish Studies minor. His poems have been anthologized in all the major collections of Jewish American poetry in recent years.

WILLIAM KLOEFKORN teaches and writes in Lincoln, Nebraska. He has authored more than a dozen collections of poetry, among them *Dragging Sand Creek for Minnows, Drinking the Tin Cup Dry*, and, most recently, *Treehouse: New & Selected Poems*, and *Welcome to Carlos*. His memoir, *This Death by Drowning*, was published in the fall of 1997. He is married to Eloise. They have four children and a pleasant assortment of grandchildren.

JEFF KNORR teaches writing and literature at Clackamas Community College in Oregon City, Oregon, where he also coedits the *Clackamas Literary Review*. His work has appeared in *Red Brick Review, Connecticut Review, Red Rock Review*, and *Oxford Magazine*, as well as others. Poems have also been anthologized by Black Buzzard Press, Native West Press, and Adrienne Lee Press. His first collection of poems, *Standing Up to the Day*, was published in 1999.

MARILYN KRYSL lives and works in the U.S. She has also worked for Mother Teresa's Sisters of Charity at the Kalighat Home for the Destitute and Dying in Calcutta and for Peace Brigade International in Sri Lanka. Her poetry collection, *Warscape with Lovers*, won the Cleveland State Poetry Center Prize in 1996. Her most recent book is a short story collection titled *How to Accommodate Men*.

DAVID LAZAR's work has appeared in *The Anchor Essay Annual: Best of 1998*, *Chelsea*, *Southwest Review*, *Denver Quarterly*, and other journals and magazines. He has four citations for "Notable Essays of the Year" from *Best American Essays*, and his work is included in the *Prose Poem: An International Journal* "best of" issue. He edited *Conversations with M. F. K. Fisher* and *Michael Powell: Interviews* and is a member of the creative writing faculty at Ohio University.

LAURENCE LIEBERMAN has published twelve books of poetry, including *Flight from the Mother Stone* and *The Regatta in the Skies: Selected Long Poems*. His poems and critical essays have appeared in most of the country's leading magazines, among them *Atlantic Monthly*, *The New Yorker*, *New Republic*, and *Sewanee Review*. He is currently professor of English at the University of Illinois, Champaign-Urbana, and poetry editor for the University of Illinois Press.

TIMOTHY LIU's first book of poems, *Vox Angelica*, received the 1992 Norma Farber First Book Award from the Poetry Society of America. Two subsequent collections are *Burnt Offerings* and *Say Goodnight*. Widely published in such journals as *Grand Street*, *Nation*, and *Paris Review*, Liu is also the editor of *Word of Mouth: An Anthology of Gay American Poetry*. He was the 1997 Holloway Lecturer at the University of California–Berkeley and currently teaches at William Paterson University in New Jersey.

RACHEL LODEN's collection *Hotel Imperium* won the Contemporary Poetry Series competition. Her chapbook, *The Last Campaign*, won the Hudson Valley Writers' Center competition, and her poems have appeared in *Paris Review*, *Antioch Review*, *New American Writing*, *Chelsea*, *Boulevard*, and *Best American Poetry 1995*. She lives in Palo Alto, California.

MONIFA LOVE is the author of *Freedom in the Dismal*, a novel, and *Provisions*, a volume of poetry. She is the director of Free Zone Productions and teaches at Florida State University, where she serves as the Ed Love Visiting Professor of Black Studies.

JOANNE LOWERY's poems have appeared in many literary magazines, including *Columbia*, *Florida Review*, *Northwest Review*, *Seneca Review*, and *River Styx*. Her fourth collection, *Double Feature*, was published in 2000. She lives in northern Indiana.

JOHN LUNDBERG holds a B.A. from the College of William and Mary and is a candidate for an M.A. in creative writing at Florida State University. His poetry has recently appeared in *Quarterly West*, *Sycamore Review*, *Iconoclast*, and *Poetry Motel*.

WALT MCDONALD was an Air Force pilot, taught at the Air Force Academy, and is now director of creative writing at Texas Tech. He has published eighteen collections of poetry and fiction, including *Blessings the Body Gave* and *The Flying Dutchman*, *Counting Survivors*, *Night Landings*, and *After the Noise of Saigon*. Three books won awards from the National Cowboy Hall of Fame. His poems have been published in such journals as *Georgia Review*, *Nation*, *Southern Review*, and *TriQuarterly*.

CAMPBELL MCGRATH is the author of three full-length collections: *Capitalism*, *American Noise*, and *Spring Comes to Chicago*. His recent awards include the Kingsley Tufts Prize, the Cohen Prize, a Guggenheim Fellowship, a Witter-Bynner Fellowship from the Library of Congress in association with the poet laureate, and a MacArthur Fellowship. McGrath teaches creative writing at Florida International University and lives in Miami Beach with his wife and two sons.

RANDALL MANN grew up in Florida and has published poems and reviews in *Antioch Review*, *Formalist*, *New Republic*, *Quarterly West*, *Salmagundi*, and elsewhere. He works as an analyst in the Office of Clinical Research at the Cancer Center of the University of California–San Francisco. He lives in San Francisco.

PETER MEINKE has published six poetry collections, the most recent being *Zinc Fingers* and *Scars*. Among his awards are the Olivet Prize, the Paumanok Award, three prizes from the Poetry Society of America, two NEA fellowships in poetry, and the Flannery O'Connor Award for his short story collection *The Piano Turner*. He retired from directing the writing workshop at Eckerd College in 1993 and since then has been writer-in-residence at the University of North Carolina–Greensboro, the University of Hawai'i, Randolph-Macon Women's College, and other schools and universities.

ORLANDO RICARDO MENES was born in Lima, Peru, to Cuban parents but has lived most of his life in Florida. He holds a B.A. and an M.A. in English from the University of Florida and a Ph.D. in creative writing from the University of Illinois at Chicago. Currently he is an assistant professor of English at the University of Dayton. His poems and translations have appeared in *Ploughshares*, *Antioch Review*, *Chelsea*, and *Seneca Review*, among others. His second collection, *Rumba Atop the Stones*, will be published in Leeds, England.

DONALD MORRILL's poems and prose have appeared in numerous magazines, including *Georgia Review*, *Creative Nonfiction*, *Southern Review*, and *North American Review*. He is a winner of the *Missouri Review* Editors' Prize for

Nonfiction and is the author of *A Stranger's Neighborhood*, a memoir, and *At the Bottom of the Sky*, a poetry collection, which won the Mid-List First Series Award.

CARISSA NEFF is a first-generation German-American, born and raised in Idaho Falls, Idaho. She spent most of her adult life traveling diligently through Asia and the Pacific Rim while living on the Micronesian island of Guam. At present, she teaches composition and rhetoric at Florida State University and is working on a collection of poems about Micronesia.

ED OCHESTER's most recent books of poetry are *Cooking in Key West*, *Snow White Horses: Selected Poems, 1973–1988*, and *The Land of Cockaigne*. He is the editor of the Pitt Poetry Series and the general editor of the Drue Heinz Literature Prize for short fiction and for many years was director of the writing program at the University of Pittsburgh. He currently teaches in the M.F.A. writing seminars at Bennington College.

STEVE ORLEN teaches at the University of Arizona in Tucson and in the low-residency M.F.A. program at Warren Wilson College. His latest book of poems is *Kisses*, and his poems have recently appeared in *Harvard Review*, *TriQuarterly*, and *Yale Review*.

ERIC PANKEY is the author of five collections of poems: *For the New Year*, which won the Walt Whitman Award from the Academy of the American Poets; *Heartwood*, *Apocrypha*, *The Late Romances*, and *Cenotaph*. His work has been supported by fellowships from the Ingram Merrill Foundation and the National Endowment for the Arts. He is professor of English at George Mason University, where he teaches in the M.F.A. program.

JACQUELINE DEE PARKER was born in New York City and grew up in New Haven, Connecticut. She is a graduate of Sarah Lawrence College and received her M.F.A. from Louisiana State University, where she works as an English instructor. A visual artist as well as a poet, Parker's mixed media paintings and collages are regularly exhibited. She lives in Baton Rouge with her husband, Dennis, and their two children, Rollie and Zoe.

DIXIE PARTRIDGE's poetry has appeared in *America*, *Borderlands*, *Commonweal*, *Georgia Review*, and the *Anthology of Magazine Verse/Yearbook of American Poetry*, 1997. Her essays have also appeared widely in national and regional journals.

RICARDO PAU-LLOSA was born in Havana in 1954 and came to the U.S. with his family in 1960. He is professor of English at Miami-Dade Community

College, Kendall Campus. He has published four books of poetry: *Sorting Metaphors* (Anhinga Poetry Prize, 1983), *Bread of the Imagined*, *Cuba*, and *Vereda Tropical*. Pau-Llosa's poems have appeared in dozens of literary magazines, including *North American Review*, *New England Review*, *Ploughshares*, and *Virginia Quarterly Review*.

ROBERT PHILLIPS's recent collections of poetry are *Breakdown Lane* and *Spinach Days*. He is former director of the creative writing program and John and Rebecca Moores Scholar at the University of Houston. His prizes include an Award in Literature from the American Academy of Arts and Letters. Three of his books have been named a Notable Book of the Year by the *New York Times Book Review*.

TODD JAMES PIERCE, a Kingsbury writing fellow, teaches fiction and contemporary American literature at Florida State University. His writing appears in books published by Viking/Penguin, Harcourt Brace, NCTE Press, as well as magazines and journals such as *The Missouri Review*, *American Short Fiction*, and *Speak*.

STANLEY PLUMLY is Distinguished University Professor at the University of Maryland. His new collection, *Now That My Father Lies Down beside Me: New and Selected Poems*, is forthcoming.

MARIANNE POLOSKEY was born in Berlin, Germany. Her poems have been recently published in *Paterson Literary Review*; *War, Literature, and the Arts*; *North River Review*; and *Medicinal Purposes Literary Magazine*. More than twenty of her poems have appeared in the *Christian Science Monitor*. On several occasions, she has been a guest on "The Poet's Corner," the monthly Fairleigh Dickinson University radio program. She lives with her husband in Englewood, New Jersey.

KEVIN PRUFER is the author of *Strange Wood*, which won the Winthrop Poetry Series. He is also editor of *The New Young American Poets* and *Pleiades: A Journal of New Writing*. His newest poems appear in *Southern Review*, *Prairie Schooner*, *Antioch Review*, *Boulevard*, and *TriQuarterly*.

WYATT PRUNTY's most recent book is *Unarmed and Dangerous: New and Selected Poems*. His poems and essays have appeared in such periodicals as *The New Yorker*, *New Republic*, *Parnassus*, *Boulevard*, and *Yale Review*. Prunty serves as Carlton professor of English at Sewanee, where he edits the Sewanee Writers' Series and where he founded and directs the Sewanee Writers' Conference.

LEROY V. QUINTANA is a native New Mexican who served in the Long Range Reconnaissance Patrol/Airborne in Vietnam from 1967 to 1968. Quintana is the author of seven books of poetry and has been the recipient of a National Endowment for the Arts grant.

LIAM RECTOR's books of poems are *The Sorrow of Architecture* and *American Prodigal*. He edited *The Day I Was Older: On the Poetry of Donald Hall*. He is director of the graduate writing seminars at Bennington College and lives in the Boston area.

JACK RIDL has taught poetry writing at Hope College for twenty-nine years. He is the author of three collections of poems and coauthor, with Peter Schakel, of *Approaching Poetry: Perspectives and Responses*. The Carnegie Foundation named him Michigan's Professor of the Year. He lives with his wife, Julie, their two cats, and their two Clumber Spaniels.

LUIS RODRIGUEZ is the author of the best-selling memoir *Always Running: La Vida Loca: Gang Days in L.A.* His books of poetry are *Poems from the Pavement*, *The Concrete River*, and his most recent, *Trochemoche*. He received a Lannan Foundation Fellowship in 1992 and lives in Chicago with his family, where he directs Tia Chucha Press.

BENJAMIN ALIRE SAÉNZ is the author of two poetry books, *Calendar of Dust* and *Dark and Perfect Angels*; a collection of stories, *Flowers for the Broken*; two novels, *Carry Me Like Water* and *The House of Forgetting*; and two bilingual children's books, *A Gift for Papa Diego* and *Grandma Fina and Her Wonderful Umbrellas*. He is a former Wallace E. Stegner Fellow, and in 1992 he won an American Book Award. He works and lives and writes in El Paso, Texas.

KATHERINE SÁNCHEZ is currently an M.F.A. student at the University of Florida. Her publishing credits include *Papyrus*, *Black Bear Review*, and *Oakland Review*.

SHEROD SANTOS is the author of three books of poetry and is a professor of English at the University of Missouri, Columbia. In 1998 Santos was awarded the 1998 B. F. Connors Long Poem Prize from the *Paris Review* for "Elegy for My Sister."

MARGOT SCHILPP's poetry has appeared or is forthcoming in *Denver Quarterly*, *American Letters and Commentary*, *Green Mountains Review*, *Gettysburg Review*, *Meridian*, *Verse*, *High Plains Literary Review*, and other journals. She currently lives in Utah, where she edits *Quarterly West*.

HEATHER SELLERS is a native of Orlando, Florida. She taught for three years at the University of Texas–San Antonio before moving to Michigan. She is currently an associate professor of English at Hope College. Her work appears in literary magazines such as *Field*, *Five Points*, and *Sonora Review*.

VIJAY SESHADRI was born in India and came to the United States in 1959 at the age of five. His poems, essays, and reviews have appeared in many magazines and anthologies, and he has received grants from the New York Foundation, Foundation for the Arts, and the National Endowment for the Arts. His poetry collection *Wild Kingdom* was published in 1996. He currently lives in Brooklyn with his wife and son and works as a magazine editor, freelance writer, and teacher of poetry at Sarah Lawrence College.

PATTY SEYBURN grew up in Detroit and has lived in Chicago, New York, Los Angeles, and Houston. She holds degrees from Northwestern University and the University of California–Irvine. She is currently completing her Ph.D. in Literature and Creative Writing at the University of Houston. She works as a freelance journalist and teaches composition and poetry in person, by mail, and by e-mail. She lives in Southern California with her husband, Eric Little.

VIVIAN SHIPLEY is editor of *Connecticut Review* and is the Connecticut State University Distinguished Professor at Southern Connecticut State University. She has a Ph.D. from Vanderbilt University. She has won the Reader's Choice Award from *Prairie Schooner*, the Lucille Medwick Award from the Poetry Society of America, and the Ann Stanford Prize from the University of Southern California. *Devil's Lane*, published in 1996, was nominated for the Pulitzer Prize. *How Many Stories?*, winner of *The Devil's Millhopper* Chapbook contest, was published in 1998.

JIM SHUGRUE, born in Chicago, Illinois, has worked as a sail-maker, a warehouseman, an editor and founder of *Hubbub*, a reviewer for the *Jazz Scene*, and a bookseller. His poems have appeared in *International Quarterly*, *Quarterly West*, *Poetry East*, *Fine Madness*, and *Another Chicago Magazine*; he also received an Oregon Arts Commission Poetry Fellowship as well as, in 1988, the Open Voice Award from the Writer's Voice Series in New York.

BARRY SILESKY's books include the biography *Ferlinghetti: The Artist in His Time*, a collection of short-short fiction (or prose poems) *One Thing That Can Save Us*, a collection of verse, *The New Tenants*, and a prize-winning collection of prose poems, *In the Ruins*. He teaches writing and literature at The School of the Art Institute of Chicago.

R. T. SMITH was born in the District of Columbia and has lived in Georgia, North Carolina, Alabama, and Virginia. His family origins in the west of Ireland contribute to his interest in Irish literature and music, and he has received literature fellowships from the NEA, the Alabama Commission of the Arts, and Arts International. His most recent books are *Trespasser* and *Split the Lark: Selected Poems*. Another collection, *Messenger*, is forthcoming. He currently edits *Shenandoah* and lives in Rockbridge County, Virginia.

DAVID STARKEY is associate professor of English at North Central College in Naperville, Illinois, and in 1999 was Fulbright professor of English at the University of Oulu in Finland. In addition to publishing several collections of poems with small presses, he has written a textbook, *Poetry Writing: Theme and Variations*, and coedited, with Richard Guzman, an anthology of Chicago literature, *Smokestacks and Skyscrapers*.

VIRGIL SUÁREZ is the author of over ten volumes of prose and poetry. Most recently he has published the collections *You Come Singing* and *In the Republic of Longing*. He also recently published a limited edition chapbook titled *Garabato Poems*. Currently at work on a novel, he lives with his family in Tallahassee, Florida, where he teaches creative writing at Florida State University.

MARK TAKSA's poems have recently appeared in *River City*, *Laurel Review*, and *Passages North*. *Cradlesong* won first prize in the 1993 National Looking Glass Poetry Chapbook Competition. His first poetry chapbook, *Truant Bather*, was published in 1986.

LAMAR THOMAS is a chef, cookbook author, writer, and pianist who holds degrees in Philosophy and English. He currently is a fusion chef working with the cuisines of the Pacific Rim and the Mediterranean. His poetry has appeared in *American Writing*, *Nerve Cowboy*, and *Clark Street*, among others.

SUSAN THOMAS lives in northern Vermont. Her poems and short stories have appeared in many journals, most recently *Nimrod*, *Columbia*, *Confrontation*, *Feminist Studies*, and *New Delta Review*. Her collection of short stories was a finalist for the 1999 Bakeless Prize from Bread Loaf/Middlebury and she is a recipient of a 1999 Artist Development Grant from the Vermont Arts Council.

WILLIAM TROWBRIDGE holds B.A. and M.A. degrees from the University of Missouri–Columbia and a Ph.D. from Vanderbilt University. His books are *Flickers, O Paradise, Enter Dark Stranger,* and *The Book of Kong.* He is coeditor of *The Laurel Review.*

SETH TUCKER, a native of Wyoming, is currently pursuing a Ph.D. at Florida State University. He received his M.A. from Northern Arizona University, where he served as poetry and fiction editor for *Thin Air.* A former Airborne Ranger who served in Panama and the Persian Gulf War, he played college basketball for San Francisco State University and enjoys chainsaw wood sculpting. His most recent publications have appeared in *The Mississippi Review, The Spoon River Review,* and *Camphorweed.*

RYAN G. VAN CLEAVE is the Anastasia C. Hoffman Poetry Fellow at the University of Wisconsin-Madison's Institute for Creative Writing. His most recent books are the poetry collection *Say Hello,* and the anthology *Clockpunchers: Poetry of America's Workplace.* His poetry has recently appeared in *The Christian Science Monitor, Quarterly West, River Styx, Southern Humanities Review,* and *TriQuarterly.*

GLORIA VANDO's works have appeared in numerous literary magazines and anthologies, among them *Kenyon Review, Seattle Review, New Letters, Stiletto One, Rampike,* and *Kansas City Out Loud II.* She received the 1991 Billee Murray Denny Poetry Prize and was a finalist in the 1992 Walt Whitman Poetry Contest and the 1989 Poetry Society of America's Alice Fay DiCastagnola Award. She is the author of *Promesas: Geography of the Impossible.*

TINO VILLANUEVA was born in Texas, and has had a diversity of work experiences ranging from migrant worker to Army supply clerk in the Panama Canal Zone. He received his B.A. in Spanish and English at Southwest Texas State University, an M.A. from SUNY–Buffalo, and a Ph.D. from Boston University. Collections of poetry he has authored are *Hay Otra Voz Poems, Shaking Off the Dark, Crónica de mis años peores,* and *Scene from the Movie Giant* (1993), which won a 1994 American Book Award.

MARCOS MCPEEK VILLATORO is the author of four books: *A Fire in the Earth* (a novel), *Walking to La Milpa: Living in Guatemala with Armies, Demons, Abrazos, and Death* (a memoir), *They Say That I Am Two* (a collection of poetry), and *The Holy Spirit of My Uncle's Cojones* (a novel). He grew up in California and Tennessee, then worked as a community organizer for several years in Guatemala, Nicaragua, and in a Latino migrant community of Alabama. After graduating from the Iowa Writers' Workshop, he moved to Los Angeles, where he holds the Fletcher Jones Endowed Chair in Creative Writing at Mount St. Mary's College.

JUDITH VOLLMER's second full-length collection of poetry, *The Door Open to the Fire*, was awarded the Cleveland State University Poetry Center Prize. She directs the writing program at the University of Pittsburgh at Greensburg and is the author of *Black Butterfly*, a chapbook, and *Level Green*. Volmer coedits the poetry magazine *5AM*.

MICHAEL WATERS is professor of English at Salisbury State University in Maryland. His six books of poetry include *Green Ash, Red Maple, Black Gum, Bountiful, The Burden Lifters,* and *Anniversary of the Air*. He has been the recipient of a Fellowship in Creative Writing from the National Endowment for the Arts, three Individual Artist Awards from the Maryland State Arts Council, and two Pushcart Prizes.

MILES GARETT WATSON was born and raised in a small town at the foothills of Arkansas's Ozark Mountains. He is a former Henry Hoyns Fellow at the University of Virginia and a former three-time University Fellow at Florida State University. His recent work has appeared in *Quarterly West, Poetry,* and *Crab Orchard Review,* and his first collection, a sonnet sequence entitled *Muzzleloader Journal,* is forthcoming.

CAROLYN BEARD WHITLOW, an associate professor of English, chairs the English Department and the creative writing concentration at Guilford College in Greensboro, North Carolina. Her poems have appeared in journals such as *Kenyon Review, Crab Orchard Review, Indiana Review,* and *13th Moon*. Her first collection of poems was *Wild Meat*. Selected as one of the ten North Carolina poets to appear on the 1997 PBS series "Poetry Live" hosted by Charles Kuralt, her most recent collection of poems is *Mean Blue*.

STEVE WILSON, whose books include *Allegory Dance* and *The Singapore Express,* was a recent Fulbright Scholar in Creative Writing in Transylvania. He has also taught and lived in Malaysia, Great Britain, and Ireland. His work has appeared in journals nationwide, as well as such recent anthologies as *What Have You Lost?* and *Best Texas Writing 2*. Wilson teaches at Southwest Texas State University.

MICHELE WOLF is the author of *Conversations during Sleep* (1997 Anhinga Prize for Poetry) and *The Keeper of Light* (1995 winner, "Painted Bride Quarterly" Poetry Chapbook Series). Her poems have appeared widely in literary journals — including *Poetry, Hudson Review,* and *Boulevard,* among others. Raised in

Florida, she holds degrees from Boston University and Columbia. She lives in New York City, where she works as a magazine writer and editor.

CAROLYNE WRIGHT has five books of poetry published, including *Premonitions of an Uneasy Guest* and *From a White Woman's Journal*; a collection of essays, *A Choice of Fidelities: Lectures and Readings from a Writer's Life*; and three volumes of poetry in translation from Spanish and Bengali. Another manuscript, *Seasons of Mangoes and Brainfire*, won the 1999 Blue Lynx Poetry Prize. After other visiting creative writing posts at Emory University, the University of Wyoming, Sweet Briar College, Ashland University, and the University of Miami, she is visiting associate professor at Oklahoma State University, teaching poetry and creative nonfiction workshops.

C. DALE YOUNG grew up in the Caribbean and south Florida. He works as a physician and is the poetry editor of *New England Review*. His first collection of poems was *The Day Underneath the Day*. His poems have appeared in *Paris Review*, *Partisan Review*, *Poetry*, *Salmagundi*, *Yale Review*, and elsewhere. He lives in San Francisco.

Permissions

Albert Goldbarth, "Gallery" and "*Shoyn Fergéssin*: 'I've Forgotten' in Yiddish," copyright © 1993 Albert Goldbarth. Both poems are reprinted from *The Gods* (Ohio State University Press) by permission of the author.

Ray Gonzalez, "Mexican" and "Under the Freeway in El Paso," copyright © 1999 Ray Gonzalez. Both poems are reprinted from *Cabato Sentora* (Boa Editions, 1999) by permission of the author.

Lilace Mellin Guignard, "Credo" appears by permission of the author.

H. Palmer Hall, "Big Thicket Requiem," first published in *Palo Alto Review*, appears by permission of the author.

Barbara Hamby, "13th Arrondissement Blues," appears by permission of the author.

Lola Haskins, "For Someone Considering Death," copyright © 1993 by Lola Haskins, is reprinted from *Hunger* (University of Iowa Press, 1993; Story Line Press, 1997), by permission of the author.

Hunt Hawkins, "East River Prison Barge," copyright © 1994 by Hunt Hawkins. Reprinted from *The Domestic Life* (University of Pittsburgh Press, 1994) by Hunt Hawkins, by permission of the University of Pittsburgh Press and the author.

Bob Hicok, "Plus Shipping," first published in *Shenandoah*, is reprinted from *Plus Shipping* (BOA Editions, 1998) by Bob Hicok. The poem appears by permission of BOA Editions and the author.

Brenda Hillman, "Loose Sugar" and "Red Fingernails," are reprinted from *Loose Sugar* (Wesleyan University Press, 1997) by Brenda Hillman and appear by permission of the author.

Jane Hirshfield, "Moment," copyright © 1999 by Jane Hirshfield, appears by permission of the author.

Paul Hoover, "California," first published in *The New Republic* and reprinted in *Best American Poetry 1997* (Scribner's), appears by permission of the author. "Two Uncertanties," first published in *The World* and selected for the Poetry Society of America's Poetry in Motion program, appears by permission of the author.

Carolina Hospital, "Distance," appears by permission of the author.

Austin Hummell, "Salt Longing," copyright © 1997 by Austin Hummell. Reprinted from *The Fugitive Kind* (University of Georgia Press, 1997) by Austin Hummell. This poem appears by permission of the University of Georgia Press and the author.

Mark Jarman, "Questions for Ecclesiastes," reprinted from *Questions for Ecclesiastes*, by Mark Jarman (Story Line Press, 1997). "Dialect" was first published in *Doubletake*. Both poems appear by permission of the author.

Larry Wayne Johns, "Postcards from Florida," appears by permission of the author.

Halvard Johnson, "Guide to the Tokyo Subway," first published in *The Florida Review*, appears by permission of the author.

Peter Johnson, "Easter, Circa 1960," copyright © 1997 by Peter Johnson. Reprinted from

Liam Rector, "David's Rumor," appears by permission of the author.

Jack Ridl, "American Suite for a Lost Daughter," first published in *Poetry*, appears by permission of the author.

Luis Rodriguez, "Running to America" and "City of Angels," appear by permission of the author.

Benjamin Alire Saénz, "Elegy Written on a Blue Cement Gravestone," appears by permission of the author.

Katherine Sánchez, "The Emigrant," first published in *Black Bear Review*, appears by permission of the author.

Sherod Santos, "Portrait of a Couple at Century's End," copyright © 1999 Sherod Santos, is reprinted from *The Pilot Star Elegies* (W. W. Norton, 1999) by permission of the author.

Margot Schilpp, "Manifesto," first published in *The Journal*, appears by permission of the author. "Poem from across the Country," appears by permission of the author.

Heather Sellers, "Underwater," appears by permission of the author.

Vijay Seshadri, "The Reappeared" and "The Refugee," reprinted from *Wild Kingdom* (Graywolf Press, 1996), appear by permission of the author and Graywolf Press.

Patty Seyburn, "Diasporadic" and "On Forgettings," appear by permission of the author.

Vivian Shipley, "Digging Up Peonies," first published in *Louisiana Literature*, appears by permission of the author. "Barbie, Madame Alexander, Bronislawa Wajs," first published in *The Alembic*, appears by permission of the author.

Jim Shugrue, "Flood Plain: The Right-of-Way," first appeared in *Calapooya Collage* and in *Small Things Screaming* (26 Books, 1995), reprinted here by permission of the author.

Barry Silesky, "Rural Particles," appears by permission of the author.

R. T. Smith, "Auger," appears by permission of the author.

David Starkey, "In Heavy Fog Outside Bishopville, South Carolina," first published in *The Chariton Review* and *Koan Americana* (Colonial Press, 1992), reprinted here by permission of the author. "Scoured" appears by permission of the author.

Mark Taksa, "The End of Soup Kitchens," first published in *Sundog: The Southeast Review*, appears by permission of the author.

Lamar Thomas, "Teshuvah," first published in *Arthur*, appears by permission of the author.

Susan Thomas, "New York Public Library," first published in *Licking River Review*, appears by permission of the author.

William Trowbridge, "Walking Back," first published in *Enter Dark Stranger* (University of Arkansas Press, 1989), appears by permission of the author and the University of Arkansas Press.

Seth Tucker, "How to Look West from Mount Pleasant, Utah," appears by permission of the author.

Index